I0022606

Frederick Reynolds

Management

A Comedy in Five Acts

Frederick Reynolds

Management
A Comedy in Five Acts

ISBN/EAN: 9783337005986

Printed in Europe, USA, Canada, Australia, Japan

Cover: Foto ©Thomas Meinert / pixelio.de

More available books at **www.hansebooks.com**

MANAGEMENT:

A COMEDY,

IN FIVE ACTS.

AS PERFORMED AT THE

THEATRE-ROYAL, COVENT-GARDEN.

By FREDERICK REYNOLDS.

THE FOURTH EDITION.

LONDON:

Printed by *A. Strahan, Printers Street;*

FOR T. N. LONGMAN AND O. REES, PATERNOSTER-ROW.

1799.

[*Price Two Shillings.*]

PROLOGUE,

WRITTEN BY MR. TAYLOR.

SPOKEN BY MR. BETTERTON.

———————

A Well-known Mufe, who labours once a-year,
And oft has found a fafe Afylum here,
Though Critic ftorms a Mother's fears excite,
With her new Offspring ventures forth to-night.
Confcious the features muft betray the Sire,
She feeks for no difguife of vain attire ;
What honeft Nature gave fhe brings to view,
And, for a kind adoption refts on you.
Yet haply now with reafon fhe appears
Opprefs'd with more than e'en maternal fears.
For fince fhe laft enjoy'd your foft'ring fmile,
A German Rival's charms have caught our Ifle.
And though fhe knows that Rival's favor'd race,
With daring force combine a foft'ning grace,
She knows, befides, that one of native breed
May always hope with Britons to fucceed :
And hence, though fafhion call her bigot-fool,
She takes no leffons from a foreign fchool —
But with a patriot pride fhe lets you know,
    " 'Tis Englifh ! Englifh, Sirs ! from top to toe !"
.While on your liberal candour we rely,
And Fafhion's rage with patriot zeal defy,
Think not our Author fees with jealous pain
Exotic merit Britifh laurels gain —
No — when to ALBION's hofpitable fhore
MISFORTUNE flies protection to implore ;
Or GENIUS darting from a diftant fphere,
That mental Comet fpreads its radiance here ;
May Britons glow with philanthropic fire,
Eager alike to cherifh and admire !

DRAMATIS PERSONÆ.

CAPTAIN LAVISH - - - MR. LEWIS.

MIST - - - - - - MR. FAWCETT.

WORRY - - - - - - MR. MUNDEN.

SIR HERVEY SUTHERLAND - MR. POPE.

ALLTRADE - - - - - MR. FARLEY.

FRANK - - - - - - MR. KLANERT.

STOPGAP - - - - - MR. SIMMONS.

GEOFFRY - - - - - MR. DAVENPORT.

MRS. DAZZLE - - - - MRS. DAVENPORT.

BETTY - - - - - - MISS LESERVE.

JULIANA - - - - - MRS. POPE.

SCENE—*The Country.*

MANAGEMENT.

ACT I.

SCENE —*A View of Sutherland-houfe, Park,
Gardens, &c.*

Enter GEOFFRY *and two other Servants.*

GEOFFRY.

COME, buftle, buftle—all to your feveral oc-
cupations.—Blefs me, who'd have thought of
Sir Hervey coming home:—go—enter the houfe,
and prepare for his reception—I'll wait his arrival
here.   [*Servants exeunt.*

Enter JULIANA.

Juliana. Good morning, good old Geoffry.—
I have once more eluded the vigilance of my perfecutor—once more ftolen forth from the caftle, pur-
pofely to vifit this fpot; and if my father hears
of it, I hope he won't be angry with me :—though
he denies me his protection, furely he will not pre-
clude me from contemplating fcenes that remind
me of him and my dear Mother !—why, what's the
matter? you feem agitated.

Geoffry. Well I may, Mifs Juliana—your father
B   is

is arrived from Italy, and I expect him here this very day.

Juliana. Expect my father!

Geoffry. Ay; after an abfence of thirteen years, I expect Sir Hervey once more at Sutherland-houfe: —look, here's his letter.

JULIANA (*fnatching the letter, reading and kiffing it*). Oh, I'm fo happy!—I fhall at laft behold, perhaps embrace him.

Geoffry. Nay, I fear otherwife; Sir Hervey is of a moft unforgiving difpofition, and the wrongs your mother put upon him were of a nature not eafily to be forgotten.

Juliana. Wrongs!—what wrongs, Geoffry? is the dark tale for ever to be concealed from me?— I am deferted by my father, and not to know the caufe!—Come, good old man! remember, you promifed you would one day tell me, and fince we are alone, and may not have another opportunity, come now—unveil the myftery—how, how did my mother wrong him?

Geoffry. Well then, to keep my word—Sir Hervey ever was, and I fear ever will be, a dupe to fafhion and its follies:—he gamed, he intrigued—and though in his heart devoted to Lady Sutherland, he forfook her and his home for fcenes of riot and diffipation.

Juliana. Unfortunate infatuation!

Geoffry. Lady Sutherland a long while bore this with fortitude and refignation; but young, beautiful, and accomplifhed, furrounded by admirers and neglected by her hufband, fhe at laft liftened to the addreffes of an artful and defigning villain, who convinced her of Sir Hervey's infidelity, and, by means of forged letters and other artifices, perfuaded her to elope with him.

Juliana. Indeed!

Geoffry.

Geoffry. 'Tis too true, madam;—but her guilt was
of fhort duration:—in a few days fhe came back to
that houfe, all penitence and fhame.—I fhall never
forget the day.—I told Sir Hervey of her return,
and he in a fit of rage and madnefs bid me fhut
the door againft her; this fhe overheard : 'twas too
much for a tender nature like hers :—fhe fled, and
foon after died—died of a broken heart!

Juliana (burfting into tears). Oh, for mercy!—
my poor, poor mother!

Geoffry. You were then but eight years old, and
till that hour the idol of Sir Hervey:—but your
likenefs to your mother foon making him wifh to
avoid you, you were removed to the caftle; where
he invefted Mrs. Dazzle with the unlimited power
of a guardian over you, and which I fear fhe has
exerted like a tyrant.

Juliana. Yes.—Sir Hervey could not mean that
I fhould be her prifoner!—But go on : he went
abroad—

Geoffry. He did — to Naples, where he has
ever fince refided : and now, what think you,
madam? do you blame the living or the
dead?

Juliana. I have no right to condemn either—but
in my mind the hufband who neglects an amiable
wife is refponfible for all the evils that enfue.—
Died of a broken heart!—oh, that he had but par-
doned her!—then he had had a wife, and I a mother to confole me!—but now————Do I indeed
refemble her?

Geoffry. You do—you do.

Juliana. Thank Heaven!—I may forgive her,
though my father never can.

Worry (fpeaking without). This way, my lad—
this way.

Juliana.

Juliana. Ha! there's Sir Hervey!—though I wiſh, you don't know how I dread to ſee him : let me be gone.

Geoffry. No, 'tis only Worry, his old faithful follower; honeſt ſoul! he and your father were foſtered by the ſame nurſe ; and, though long ſince in eaſy independent circumſtances, he ſtill follows Sir Hervey from motives of affection.—Suppoſe you aſk him to be a mediator for you.

Juliana. Not now—another time, another time —I muſt return to my priſon :—but though I ſhed tears over the fate of my mother, don't fancy I upbraid my father.—No! I feel for both—and let him ſtill avoid, ſtill puniſh and abandon me, I know his motive : and the fond hope that he will one day prove a parent to me, will make me bear even greater ills with patience.—Oh! may that day be not far off! for 'twill be the proudeſt and the happieſt of my life.   [*Exit.*

Enter WORRY *and a* Servant.

Worry. Mind, do as I order you ; when the baggage arrives let me know. (*Exit Servant.*) What Geoff!—give me your hand, old Geoff!—Sir Hervey is but a ſtage behind.—'Slife! I thought we ſhould never ſhake hands again.

Geoffry. So did I ; 'tis thirteen years (*ſhaking hands and looking hard at Worry*) ; but, heyday! how you are altered, Maſter Worry!

Worry. Yes, i'm not the ſame man I was.

Geoffry. So I ſee ; but how has it happened?

Worry. I don't know—I lead a different ſort of life—I think ; and I'm afraid I drink a great deal.

Geoffry. You drink! you that uſed to be the moſt temperate, ſober——

Worry.

Worry. Ay; and I ufed to hate cards, you know; now I could play all day :—I ufed to break appointments; now I come an hour before my time; —and I that always laid in bed ti!l noon, now conftantly rife with the crowing of the cock.

Geoffry. Why, what the deuce, are you mad?

Worry. No—I'm married.—I've got a loving jealous wife!—and whilft Sir Hervey is continually miferable becaufe Lady Sutherland ran away from him, here am I——I tell you what, Geoff—if Mrs. Worry were to run away from me, I'm fure I fhould be too much of a philofopher to repine on the occafion.

Geoffry. What! and is Sir Hervey likewife altered?—or does he ftill go on rioting in diffipation and extravagance?

Worry. Worfe and worfe—only yefterday he employed Mr. Alltrade to raife five thoufand pounds for him on his bond—offered a premium of fifty *per cent.* and the moment he receives the money, away it will go in galas or at the gaming table—No, I beg pardon—not at the gaming table—now-a-days no money ever goes there.

Geoffry. What! have they left off playing?

Worry. No—but they've left off paying;—and that's the reafon the faro banks are knocked up—when people only play for love, friendfhip won't induce them to keep open houfe.—But Mifs Sutherland—there's Sir Hervey's greateft plague. A meeting with her was his chief motive for leaving Italy, and now we underftand fhe vindicates her mother, and takes part againft him.

Geoffry. She is belied, cruelly belied!

Worry. Nay; we have it from the beft authority, —Mrs. Dazzle—the lady who brought her up, and for whom I have a meffage—but of this be

affured,

affured, Geoff; Sir Hervey's cafe isn't half fo defperate as mine:—he's only tormented by a daughter who will try to break his heart, but I've got a jealous wife, who will actually break my head, heart, and purfe ftrings.

Re-enter Servant.

Servant. Sir, the baggage is come.

Worry. You hear—Mrs. Worry is arrived.— Come, will you go and be introduced ?

Geoffry. With all my heart—but mind now— you'll one day find that Mrs. Dazzle has traduced Mifs Sutherland, and only becaufe fhe was a great favourite of her late hufband's. He was a diftant relation, you know, and I did hope would have remembered her in his will—but no—he, like the reft of her family—he—has forgotten her !

Worry. To be fure ; who ever got any good by thefe diftant relations? Mrs. Worry has a little thoufand ; and do you know my apartments are fo conftantly cram'd with coufins, neices, uncles, aunts, and grandmothers, that at dinner-time I never get a chair to fit upon—I eat flying !—And talk of the comforts of a fire-fide, curfe me if I've been within ten yards of mine fince the day I was married :—not that I complain of cold though— my houfe is warm enough, I promife you :—but come along; and forry am I to be convinced of Mifs Sutherland's ingratitude.—Were fhe the girl you defcribe, I would not only be her friend and advocate, but if Sir Hervey refufed to protect her, I would myfelf be a father to her. [*Exeunt.*

SCENE—*An Apartment in the Caſtle.*

Enter Mrs. DAZZLE *and* BETTY.

Betty. Even ſo, ma'am; Miſs Juliana fiſt robbed you of your huſband's friendſhip, and now of the Captain's love.

Mrs. Dazzle, Oh, the little viper!—but I know how to be amply revenged:—the great objeſt of her life is a reconciliation with her father;—this I have already prevented, and will ſtill prevent.—But the Captain, Betty—do you think he has ſerious views?

Betty. He ſerious! what Captain Laviſh prefer Juliana Sutherland without a ſhilling, to the widow Dazzle with a nett eſtate of five thouſand a-year!

Mrs. Dazzle. That's true:—I married little Jerry for his fortune, and I am certainly ſole heireſs—to be ſure I hav'nt yet ſeen the will, becauſe he died in London:—but I expeſt his agent Mr. Alltrade with it every moment, and then, Betty!—poor Juliana!—I hope the Captain will allow her half pay.

Betty. Oh you're too liberal, ma'am—but ſee! here comes Mr. Alltrade with the will.

Enter ALLTRADE.

Alltrade. Well! madam, as good as my word, you ſee:—this moment arrived with my friend Sir Hervey.

Mrs. Dazzle. You are very kind, Mr. Alltrade; but there was no occaſion to be in any hurry—every body knows how little Jerry loved me.

Alltrade. Oh, there's no doubt that the will is completely in your favour; but you had better open it, leſt there ſhould be any ſmall bequeſt or legacies—

Mrs. Dazzle. Well, to oblige you I'll juſt caſt my eye over it—(*takes the will from* ALLTRADE)

B 4 Poo·

Poor Jerry!—he uſed to ſay he ſhould fall a martyr
to love. (*Reads will*): " By this my laſt will, I
" Jeremiah Dazzle give and bequeath all the pro-
" perty of which I die poſſeſſed unto that moſt
" lovely and accompliſhed of her ſex"——Spare
me—ſpare a poor widow's bluſhes, Mr. Alltrade.

Alltrade. Nay! it's not more than you deſerve.

Mrs. Dazzle. Oh, Sir! (*curtſeying—then reads
on :*)—" unto that moſt lovely and accompliſhed of
her ſex, Juliana Sutherland"—Juliana!—why, Mr.
Alltrade! (*Half crying.*)

Alltrade. Go on.

Mrs. Dazzle (*reads on*).   " Juliana Suther-
" land, whom being deſerted by her father, I take
" a pride in adopting. But my will further is, that
" ſhe hold the ſaid property no longer than ſhe re-
" mains unmarried. In caſe ſhe marries, I give the
" ſame to my widow Deborah Dazzle. And my
" only motive for thus tying up my couſin Juliana,
" is to ſave her from entering into a ſtate to which
" I feil a martyr."——Why it's a forgery! he
could not—dared not!

Alltrade. Nay—there's no doubt that it's genu-
ine—but be compoſed—doesn't Miſs Sutherland
live in this houſe?

Mrs. Dazzle. She does.

Alltrade. Then it dawns! it glares upon me!—
Mark—if ſhe marries, the eſtate devolves to you—
are not theſe Mr. Dazzle's words!

Mrs. Dazzle. They are: and I only wiſh I had
been behind him when he wrote them!

Alltrade. Well: be patient—don't deſtroy the
will, becauſe that's a ſerious buſineſs (*pulling up
his neckcloth*):—only conceal it till you get Juliana
a huſband—then ſhe forfeits the legacy, and you
become heireſs to a hundred thouſand pounds.

Mrs.

Mrs. Dazzle. Why that looks well—but how?
——the Captain won't marry her.

Alltrade. No, but I will; in the firſt place her
being in this houſe will give me numberleſs oppor-
tunities; and in the next I am employed by Sir
Hervey to raiſe five thouſand pounds for him on
his bond—now if we can get Juliana to join in it,
I ſhall have them both ſo completely in my power,
that if I fail in the character of a lover, I may
ſucceed in that of a creditor :—you underſtand.

Mrs. Dazzle. I do—excellent!—and as a reward for your trouble—

Alltrade. I only aſk a third of the eſtate.

Mrs. Dazzle. Granted—it is a bargain.

Alltrade. Say you ſo ?—then let's to work inſtantly—and look here comes one who, from his
influence over Sir Hervey, we muſt ſecure as a
confederate.

Enter WORRY.

Mrs. Dazzle. Worry, my old acquaintance!—
I give you joy of your marriage, and ſincerely wiſh
you may never know the pangs of widowhood.

Alltrade. And ſo do I with all my heart,
Worry.

Worry. And I wiſh with all my ſoul you'd both
keep your wiſhes to yourſelves. (*Aſide.*)—But I wait
upon you, madam, from Sir Hervey :—from your
account of Miſs Sutherland's undutiful and indiſ-
creet conduct, he perſiſts in not ſeeing her, and
therefore while he ſtays in the country, he begs
ſhe may be more cloſely confined than ever.

Mrs. Dazzle. I'll do all I can; but ſhe is ſo artful and deſigning, that for my part I don't think
ſhe'll ever be ſafe till ſhe gets a huſband to protect her.

Alltrade.

Alltrade. Nor I; and I'll tell you a fecret, Worry—I love her, and wifh to be that hufband: and fince, from my humble birth and inferior fituation, I cannot afpire to gaining Sir Hervey's confent, will you aid and affift the marriage?

Worry. With all my heart—the more matches the better.—When one's in a fcrape onefelf, nothing's fo confoling as to fee all one's friends in the fame fituation. *(Afide.)* I'll affift you—but about the bond—have you raifed the five thoufand pounds.

Alltrade. No; and I defpair of fuccefs—the friend I applied to wants Mifs Sutherland to join.

Worry. She join! why fhe's as poor——

Alltrade. I know—but he fays fhe has rich relations—may have a handfome legacy—in fhort, it will mend the fecurity:—therefore let Sir Hervey know this, and he will fee the necefity of commanding her to fign inftantly. *(*WORRY *is going.)*

Mrs. Dazzle. Good day, Worry—I fhall be always glad to fee you: and becaufe there's a hatchment over my door, don't fancy this is abfolutely the houfe of mourning.

Worry. No, ma'am;—I—I—*(laughing and trying to conceal it).*

Mrs. Dazzle. Why, what do you laugh at?—fpeak out—you won't offend me.

Worry. Shan't I, ma'am?—then begging your pardon, you need'nt have caution'd me; for I always look on a hatchment outfide of a widow's houfe like a fign over an inn—a certain emblem of revelry and good cheer.—And when I'm a widower—oh! oh! oh! *(fhakes his head, fighs, and exit)*

Alltrade. So far, fo well; he's in our intereft—but to get this bond out of Sir Hervey's hands, we muft at leaft advance a few hundreds, and where to raife even thofe—for my part I haven't a guinea.

Mrs,

Mrs. Dazzle. Nor I now a shilling !—*(sighing)* nor do I know where to raise one ?

Alltrade. No !

Mrs. Dazzle. No ; unless indeed Mr. Mist the manager of our country theatre—

Alltrade. What ! the quondam silversmith of Cheapside !—he's an old friend of mine,

Mrs. Dazzle, Is he ?—then you may aid my suit.—You must know, smitten with the love of fame, eager to acquire the reputation of wit and genius, I have written a most magnificent play, which of course I am all anxiety to see acted ; he has already promised to come and read it, and if it meets with his approbation, very likely he may advance the money necessary to pay Sir Hervey.

Alltrade. True—suppose I hasten his visit—I'll seek him instantly ; and whilst you keep Juliana out of sight, I'll keep the will out of sight—*(putting will in his pocket).*—And with regard to the play, if you get money by it, depend on't you'll get reputation also ; one generally follows the other.

Mrs. Dazzle. So it does—and how the case is alter'd ?—formerly wits had no money, and now he that has no money has no wit ; for whilst a bad joke will be applauded from the head of a great able, a good one will be lost if spoken by him who has nothing but wit to recommend him !—but away to the manager—let the war begin, and doubt not our victory !   [*Exeunt.*

SCENE—*Outside of the Theatre.*

Enter STOPGAP (*from the Box-office*).

Stopgap. Pooh—I'll fit there picking my teeth no longer;—ftay for ever, there won't be a place taken; for well as Mr. Mift might underftand conducting a fhop, he knows fo little how to manage a theatre, that during the time I have been prompter, treafurer, box-book-keeper, and deputy manager, there have been only three boxes taken— and they were by particular friends, who thought they did him an honour by coming in with orders ——pfha!—I'll go——heh?—who's here?—aha? a flat at laft!

Enter ALLTRADE.

Stopgap. This way, Sir,—there's the office—have a front row in any part of the houfe, Sir—

Alltrade. Sir, I want to fpeak to Mr. Mift— where is he? (STOPGAP *holds down his head*).— Why don't you anfwer me?—where can I find him?

Stopgap. He's walking on the London road— you'll find him there, all anxiety, looking out for the new Harlequin whom we expect every hour by the flow waggon.

Alltrade. Expect Harlequin by the flow wag- gon!

Stopgap. Yes, Sir: and between you and me, 'tis high time he came; we play to fhocking houfes— laft night to Hamlet we were obliged to make a fhew, by fhoving the band into the pit, the orange women into the boxes, and the door-keepers into the galleries.——Indeed no wonder at it, for Mr. Mift himfelf played Hamlet.

Alltrade.

Alltrade. The old tradefman act Hamlet!

Stopgap. Even fo—he always will act the beft part—but here he comes, and fpite of the bad houfes, all buftle, life, and animation!

Enter MIST.

Mift. Damn that flow waggon—not here 'till feafon's over—however, fure of tol lol houfe to night—fine day—ftrong bill—nothing againft— what Jack! Jack Alltrade!—why what brings you to this—— oh! oh!—fly dog!—written a Farce— can't get it acted in London—and fo come——

Alltrade. Not I upon my honour.

Mift. Want an engagement then!—what's your line? Ben, Scrub, and Calliban; or Richard, Romeo, and the tiptops—no difference though—tragedy or comedy—play which you will, Jack—fure to en- tertain audience—he! he! he!

Alltrade. Why 'Slife—here's an alteration!— when I laft faw you, you were leaving off trade with a capital fortune, and retiring into the country free from the cares and vexation of bufinefs.

Mift. Hem! much you know of the matter— when I loft care and vexation, loft my two beft friends.

Alltrade. Care and vexation your beft friends!

Mift. Yes: couldn't tell what to do with myfelf —all day long watching clock, or yawning at ftreet door—could'nt bear it—hardly alive—thought of opening new fhop—when one lucky day!—play houfe put up at auction—always had theatrical twift—fo bid handfomely—knock'd down at large fum to be fure—but what then? been happy ever fince—had care and vexation in abundance—but

mum——

mum—fhan't ftop here—London—Covent Garden
—Drury Lane—they're my object!

Alltrade. Indeed!—then why not make them
your object now?—why not engage London players?

Mift. Um! *(fnapping his fingers)*—that for
London players—and that for London authors—
foon have beft actor and fineft writer living—heh:
know who I mean? *(mimics Harlequin.)* ·

Alltrade. Harlequin!

Mift. Right—back his wooden fword againft
their wooden heads—bring all Europe—young and
old boys—little babies, and full grown babies:—and
then for falary—only twelve fhillings a week, and
fare of flow waggon—whereas thefe London gentlemen, with their ten pounds a night and poft
chaifes and four——befides, won't do here?—don't
I come from London?—don't I act Hamlet, and
to what?—not enough to pay the lighting?—but
can't ftay—muft go look after the tricks—muft
get all fmooth 'gainft great man's arrival.

Alltrade. Nay: I've an invitation for you—
Mrs. Dazzle is extremely anxious about her play,
and requefts you'd wait upon her.

Mift. I wait!—who's manager?—befides d——d
ftuff I fuppofe.

Alltrade. That I can't fay—but when I tell you,
fhe is a lady I have the greateft regard for——

Mift. Enough—come this evening—be there
before doors open—till when, in the words of
Hamlet, Remember me!

Alltrade. Hamlet!—in the words of the Ghoft,
you mean.

Mift. Yes: but when I act Hamlet, play the
Ghoft too—always take every good fpeech in the

play

play and whip into my part—I'm manager—
he! he! he!

Alltrade. Well, adieu—and after the reading,
I'll look in at the theatre.

Mift. Do—fhan't coft you a farthing—put you
in at ftage door, and fit in my box—Strong bill to-
night—Beggar's Opera in two acts—Filch by a
gentleman of the law, being his firft and laft appearance on any ftage—after which, a grand fpec-
tacle of my own writing, called " Gulliver the
" Great."—In the firft act, all the characters will
be killed—in the fecond, introduced their execu-
tors, adminiftrators, and affigns—but come and
judge.——I fay though, when new pantomime
comes out, trouble you not to walk about the
town, Jack.

Alltrade. Why?

Mift. Why!—who'll pay to look at my clown,
when they can fee you for nothing—he! he! he!
—come along, Stop.   [*Exeunt.*

THE END OF THE FIRST ACT.

ACT II.

SCENE—*Outſide of the Caſtle.*

Enter Sir HERVEY SUTHERLAND, WORRY, *and*
GEOFFRY.

Sir Hervey. 'Sdeath! how mortifying! how
perplexing!—and yet, without the money, inevit-
able ruin follows. Are you ſure that was Mr.
Alltrade's meſſage?

Worry. Yes, Sir; he cannot raiſe the five
thouſand pounds unleſs Miſs Juliana joins in the
bond.

Sir Hervey. Well, be it ſo.—Enter the caſtle
inſtantly, and tell her 'tis by my command; the
firſt and laſt requeſt her father ever will make to
her—begone—[WORRY *exit*].—And now, old
man, obey my orders—let there be maſks and
dancing—I cannot encounter ſolitude—that leads
to thought, and thought engenders madneſs; and
I muſt plunge 'midſt any ſpecies of ſociety to ſave
me from myſelf: therefore, let the doors of Su-
therland-houſe once more be opened, and let revelry and good cheer welcome my return.

Geoffry. I ſhall obey, Sir.

Sir Hervey. Give general invitation to my
friends.

Geoffry. Your friends!—Oh, I'm glad of that,
Sir—then I hope I know one who will be of the
party.

Sir

Sir Hervey. Indeed! who, Geoffry?

Geoffry. With fubmiffion, Mifs Juliana, Sir—don't be angry—but if the title of friend admits any one into your houfe, in my mind none ought to be more welcome than your own daughter.

Sir Hervey. How!—have a care, Sir.

Geoffry. Nay, you are deceived, cruelly deceived; fhe has no hope, no wifh beyond you: only this very morning, with tears in her eyes, fhe exclaimed, " The day that reconciles me to my " father will be the proudeft and the happieft of " my life!"—Thefe were her words—and now, to fee her imprifoned!——(*pointing to the caftle.*)

Sir Hervey (much agitated). Did fhe—did fhe fay this, Geoffry?

Geoffry. She did, Sir—and at the fame time fhe put on fuch a fweet fafcinating look—exactly fuch a one as her late mother——

Sir Hervey. Who, Sir?

Geoffry. Such a one as poor Lady Sutherland, Sir,——

Sir Hervey. Diftraction!—you've raifed the latent fury here; and I would fooner prefs a viper to my breaft than the image of a woman who had fo wronged me.—I'll hear no more—befides, this is all artifice—I've been informed how well fhe loves her father; and for the imprifonment you talk of, I fanction and approve it.—Better be even cloiftered thus, than only come into the world to vindicate and fhare a falfe, falfe mother's crimes.

Geoffry. What! can Mrs. Dazzle be bafe enough——

Sir Hervey. Peace, old man—on pain of your difmiffal utter not a word againft that beft of women and of friends.—Attend me home, and

c   inftantly

inſtantly make preparation for ſplendid hoſpi-
tality.—(*Going.*)

Geoffry. Look, Sir!—only look!—there's poor
Miſs Juliana ſitting at her priſon window!—ſee,
how innocent and how melancholy ſhe appears!—
Suppoſe now you were juſt to ſtay and—and—
ſpeak to her, Sir.

Sir Hervey. I ſpeak!—away!—lead not my
mind to thoughts that madden whilſt they charm
me—No—in the huſband's wrongs I'll bury all the
fond, fond feelings of the father.—(*Going, Geoffry
ſtops him.*)

Geoffry. Nay, Sir, only turn and take one look
at her——

Sir Hervey. I dare not—I dare not—(*ruſhes
out, followed by Geoffry*).

SCENE—*An Apartment in the Caſtle.*

Enter JULIANA.

Juliana. Oh, what a fate is mine!—a father,
whom I haven't ſeen from infancy, and now ſo near
me—and I'm denied the ſight of him—nay more,
am told that, by his orders, this place is ſtill to be
my priſon.—Oh, my mother! I feel my heart, like
yours, can't long ſupport it.—(*Weeps.*)—I ſhall
ſoon follow thee!

Enter WORRY.

Worry. So, there ſhe is—what a frightful, undutiful countenance!—Oh, ſhe'll ſee us all ſtarve
before——Madam!

Juliana. As I live, the man that Geoffry ſpoke
of—what can he want?—(*Advances towards him.*)
—May I aſk—I hope Sir Hervey's well?

Worry.

Worry. No, he's very ill, I'm very much obliged to you.

Juliana. Ill !—heavens!——what's his complaint ?

Worry. An ungrateful daughter!——Your pardon, ma'am—perhaps I'm fomewhat blunt—but I have lived with Sir Hervey thefe twenty years : if he has faults to others, he has none to me; and though the world deferts him, it is my duty to ftand or fall with him.

Juliana. Well, I applaud your zeal; but why, why charge me with ingratitude ?

Worry. Becaufe you are his enemy; becaufe you take the part of her who bafely wrong'd him.

Juliana. Hold, cenfure me as much as you pleafe; but breathe not a fyllable againft my mother.

Worry. There ! you avow it; you juftify——

Juliana. No—but I feel for her; I lament her fate : that confolation Sir Hervey cannot deny me. —And let him know me before he condemns me; for how can that child be called ungrateful who never had an opportunity of evincing either her duty or affection ?

Worry. How!

Juliana. I never wronged him; and even in my infancy he fhut his doors againft me.—I am his child; and by denying his protection, he has expofed me to the felf-fame fnares my mother fell a martyr to.—I've not difgraced—I've ever loved him : and let him give me but the trial—oh ! let him take me to his heart; and if the careffes of an affectionate daughter do not atone for the errors of a mifguided mother, then let him caft me from him; but till then let him not accufe me of ingratitude.

C 2 *Worry.*

Worry. What! and you'd——how handfome·
fhe looks!—you'd be loving and dutiful?

Juliana. Oh yes—I'd watch, I'd nurfe him—
weep as he wept, and blefs each fmile that cheered
him : and when time had mellowed his grief into a
fweet remembrance of my mother's lofs, then I'd
retrieve her honour in the grave :—in my un-
varied truth, all, all fhould be forgotten. I would
revive the friendfhip that he bore her, and fhe
fhould live again in Juliana.

Worry. Blefs my foul!—now only think of my
not marrying fuch a woman!—and if he wanted
money, and you had it to lend him——

Juliana. If I had millions, I would devote them
all to him.

Worry. Old Geoff's right.—May I never go to
Heaven if fhe isn't an angel!—and if the widow
isn't fomething elfe, may I go fomewhere elfe.

Juliana. Ay, Mrs. Dazzle; fhe is my perfecutor: from the hour I accidentally interfered with
her in Captain Lavifh's affection, fhe——

Worry. Captain Lavifh!—what, your father's
antagonift—the man who two years ago fought
him in Switzerland?

Juliana. Alas! the fame.

Worry. And did you return his affection?

Juliana. What could I do?—he rifked his own
life to fave mine—'tis but a fhort and fimple tale—
One day, when I had liberty to ride within the pre-
cincts of the caftle, my horfe ran away with me,
and he in ftopping it broke his arm: I could do
no lefs than confefs the obligation; and fince his
recovery, often vifiting Mrs. Dazzle, our intimacy
encreafed, and gratitude grew into love.

Worry. And all the time did you know of the
duel?

Juliana.

Juliana. No; till yefterday I never heard of it; and then I inftantly informed him, that though Sir Hervey neglected his duty to me, I could never forget mine to him, and nothing fhould induce me to receive that man as a lover, who defigned to be the murderer of my father. (WORRY *croffes her as if going*)—Why, what's the matter?—where are you going?

Worry. To Sir Hervey; to bid him remove you from the protection of a hypocrite, and place you under his own.

Juliana. Oh, will you—will you be fo generous? Indeed in this caftle I am not fafe a moment.

Worry. No—nor any body elfe; for the roof will tumble in to a certainty; but I'll go directly: and if I fail, and the war continues—let the enemy look to it—I've ferved many a hard campaign, and though not lately in the battles abroad, thanks to Mrs. Worry I've feen pretty warm fervice at home; and fooner than you fhould remain under the rod of a tyrant, I'd ftorm the caftle, and revive the age of chivalry:—yes—I would—I " Will Worry," the married man!—So retire, and wait my coming, madam—I'll not be long.

Juliana. I'm fure you will not: and pray remind my father, that I have fuffered in my turn; that we are partners in calamity, and by meeting we might divide and diffipate each other's woes.—Tell him—but you know my thoughts, and to your conduct I commit a caufe on which my hope, my happinefs, my life depends! [*Exeunt.*

SCENE—*Another Apartment in the Caſtle*, Mrs.
DAZZLE *and* MIST *diſcovered ſitting at a Table—*
MIST *with a Manuſcript in his Hand.*

Mrs. Dazzle. Now then, Mr. MIST—now begin
the play : but remember, I haven't quite finiſhed it.

Miſt (reading). " *Mary Queen of Scots, a grand*
" *heroic drama ; with new ſcenes, new dreſſes, new*
" *decorations, new*"—hem : that's my affair—I'm
manager———

Mrs. Dazzle. Oh, certainly, Sir ———

Miſt (reading). " *Scene the firſt—a room in a*
" *Caſtle—the Duke of Norfolk diſcovered with a key*
" *in his hand. The Duke*—Now, by my holy dame,
" with this ſame key, Jockey of Norfolk, thou'lt
" unlock the gate of Scottiſh Mary's priſon !—*He*
" *unlocks the gate and leads forth Mary.*—Beſhrew
" me, but your ſafe, and ſo good morrow, good
" Queen Elizabeth !"—(MIST *lays down the play,*
and riſes:) Won't do—won't bring ſixpence—refuſe
it— I refuſe it!

Mrs. Dazzle. How! why I flattered myſelf I
had caught the true Shakſperian fire.

Miſt. And ſuppoſe you had—what then ?—played
Hamlet laſt night under ten pounds ; and I ſay
that's a bad play that brings a bad houſe.—Harlequin and Abraham Newland—they're the only pulling writers, except indeed the Germans ; and
there!—there I'm beforehand with the Londoners—
mum--mine's a German Harlequin—he !—he !—
However, try another page—if that's not better,
don't you finiſh play—audience will finiſh it for
you. (*Reads play :*)

" *Enter*

" *Enter Queen Elizabeth and Burleigh.*——*The*
" *Queen*—Go to—we'll nip'em i'the bud.—Why,
" how now, rebels?—for this treacherous queen,
" convey her to the tower—and there, good Bur-
" leigh—You take the hint—Away! —Burleigh
" *carries off* Mary *and*"——(*here* Mist *is inter-*
rupted by loud rattling at stage door)—You hear—
applause interrupts us.

Mrs. Dazzle. Who can it be?—dear! was there
ever any thing fo unlucky?

Mist. Not at all; for this relief much thanks—
(*taking up his hat and cane*).—Decided, in my
opinion—firft night difapprobation—fecond, under
expences—third, nobody but the author.—Yours,
devotedly yours.

Mrs. Dazzle. Nay, I infift you don't ftir (*noife at
door again*).—You hear!—do only be kind enough
to ftep into the next room, and I'll get rid of this in-
trufive perfon in a moment: come now, indulge an
anxious author; and confider though it don't read,
it may act well.

Mist. That's true; nothing reads worfe than
pantomime; but in reprefentation!—Oh gods! and
goddeffes!—give me the manufcript—I'll indulge
you (*takes the play*)—one—two—only four acts!—
never mind—if play's bad, lefs of bad thing the
better—if good, I and my copyift foon cobble up
fifth act for you—but I'm gone—(*Going, returns*)
Mum! ever fee Gulliver the Great?—that was our
writing—to be fure audience damn'd it the firft
night, but what then?—Theatre's mine!—fo gave
'em a dofe of it; acted it fifty nights running—revenged myfelf there—he! he! he!—and in like
manner always will maintain dignity!—always, as
long as I'm P. M., Peter Mill—and M. P.
manager of a play houfe! [*Exit.*
Mrs.

Mrs. Dazzle. Now then, for this tormentor——
(*opens door, and enter* JULIANA).—You Mifs!—how
dare you——

Juliana. Oh, madam!—I'm fo terrified!—even
now, Mr. Alltrade, a total ftranger, propofed marriage to me; and told me that, aided by his own
merit and your intereft, he didn't doubt of fuccefs,
—Nay, on my refufing him, he abfolutely threatened
to ufe force.

Mrs. Dazzle. And on this account you fled from
him?

Juliana. I did, madam: and I entreat you to
protect and fave me.

Mrs. Dazzle. Bafe, worthlefs girl!—then know
Mr. Alltrade fpoke truth; he is the man I have
felected for your hufband.

Juliana. Heavens! and can you mean——

Mrs. Dazzle. I mean you fhould be his wife!
and till you confent, your chamber fhall be your
prifon—

Juliana (*falling at her feet*). Oh, for mercy!
—Look at me—I am friendlefs, fatherlefs!

Mrs. Dazzle. And who have you to thank for
it?—Yes: 'tis as I faid—Captain Lavifh has taught
you to defpife marriage, and copy the example of
her who made you fatherlefs.

Juliana. What! do you allude to——

Mrs. Dazzle. I do—and beware, Mifs—dare not
to imitate fuch falfe, abandoned conduct.

Juliana. Abandoned!

Mrs. Dazzle. Ay: would you juftify it?—have
you the audacity to vindicate deeds the moft licentious!—actions——

Juliana (*rifing*). Were you the being that I
moft refpect—were you my father!—I'd tell you
it is falfe!—Licentious!—oh, had my illfated mother
                                                    poffeffed

possessed one atom that resembled you, I'd tear her image from my heart, or die!

Mrs. Dazzle. Take care, or——

Juliana. Oh, shame! shame!—is this the protection I might expect from one of my own sex?—Men would betray us; let us not betray each other! and while she whom you censure might meet with pity and forgiveness, what can the female seducer expect?—the scorn of one sex, the abhorrence of the other.

Mrs. Dazzle. Begone!—retire to your chamber—nay, no reply;—I will be obeyed—(*walks up the stage in a rage*).

Enter WORRY.

Juliana (*running hastily up to him*). Oh! have you seen my father?—will he, will he take pity on me?

Worry. Alas, madam!—I can do nothing for you.

Juliana. What! he persists!

Worry. Most obstinately : he says your offer of advancing money is no more than your duty, and what a parent has a lawful claim to.

Juliana. Then may he feel——but he's deceived, and I forgive him.

Mrs. Dazzle (*coming down stage*). Not gone yet!—Do as I command : to your chamber I insist —(*takes* JULIANA *by the arm and leads her to stage* . *door*—JULIANA *exit.*)—And you, Worry, as you've kindly undertaken to assist Mr. Alltrade, go to him instantly ; tell him Miss Sutherland has so grossly insulted me, that I've no longer any conscientious scruples, and if he chooses to secure the marriage by carrying her off——

Worry.

Worry. Carrying her off!

Mrs. Dazzle. Ay:. force will be the ſhorteſt mode: ſo bid him come in a poſt-chaiſe to the weſtern gate, whilſt I go and make ſure of my priſoner.—Away—loſe not a moment, and tell him I'll anſwer for the ſucceſs of the enterprize. [*Exit*.

Worry. I go to Mr. Alltrade!—I aid—bleſs my ſoul!—No wonder ſhe's a widow—If ſhe married every morning, her huſband would die before night: —but I will aid in carrying her off—I'll go di- rectly and get aſſiſtance—I'll entreat the firſt man I meet to join with me :—and let Sir Hervey con- demn, or, what's more tremendous, let Mrs. Worry ſcold me, I know I'm doing my duty!—So in ſpite of wives, widows, and devils, I'll ſecure her eſcape, and ſtill try to reſtore her to her father. (*Going*.)

Re-enter MIST (*with the Play in his hand*).

Miſt. Oh, it won't do--'twill be damn'd.

Worry. Now pray take pity—pray give your aſſiſtance, Sir :—there's the ſweeteſt young lady juſt lock'd into that room, and if you would but help to releaſe her——

Miſt. How! what! young lady lock'd up! and I help to releaſe her !—pooh—nonſenſe!—what's her caſe !—And me—why apply to me ?

Worry. Becauſe I'm ſure you will befriend us— and if you did but know how well ſhe had con- ducted herſelf!—how charmingly ſhe had acted her part—

Miſt. What ! acted her part !

Worry. Ay ! no woman ever acted better :— ſuch ſenſe ! ſuch feeling, Sir !—and now, when ſhe is ſo ready to engage herſelf—

Miſt. Ready to engage !—oh, ho—comprehend now—lock'd up to keep her from the ſtage, and
                                                        apply

apply to me 'caufe I'm Manager—he! he!—Hark
ye; how's her voice?

Worry. Delightful.

Mift. And her action?

Worry. Graceful.

Mift. And her figure?

Worry. Beautiful.

Mift. Damme fhe'll do my bufinefs till Harlequin comes! Say no more—my houfe is open—
I'll give her an appearance.

Worry. What!—you'll get her out!

Mift. To be fure I will—in what part fhe likes beft
—tragedy, comedy, opera, farce, pantomime!—
And you!—want a clown—you fhall play clown—
alfo if you're married! don't reply—fee it by your
chin—give you and your wife freedom—perpetual
free admiffion.—But now for it—now to plan plot
——Hem!—Here is the author.

Enter (from folding doors) Mrs. DAZZLE.

*Mrs. Dazzle (locking doors and putting the key
in her pocket).* So now Juliana's fafe, and I get my
hufband's eftate.—Oh, Worry, have you feen Mr.
Alltrade?

Worry (confufed). Hey! yes—I've feen Mr.
Alltrade, and he'll be here with the chaife directly.

Mift (reading play). " Burleigh carries off
Mary."

Mrs. Dazzle. What! no further, Mr. Mift?—
I fuppofe you're thinking of the effect, Mr. Manager?

Worry. Mr. Manager!—Oh! I underftand
now—

Mift. Yes; but can't tell without rehearfal—
cannot judge unlefs I faw it on the boards—Let me
fee—there's the prifon gate—*(pointing to folding
doors)*:

doors):—you are Jockey Norfolk—no I'm Jockey
——I'll tell you what—fuppofe we give it a trial!

Mrs. Dazzle. A trial! what a rehearfal now in
this room?—Delightful!—I fhould like it of all
things.

Mifs. So fhould I—then liften—I'll play Norfolk—you Queen Elizabeth —

Mrs. Dazzle. He, Burleigh—(*pointing to*
Worry).

Worry. Who the devil's Burleigh.—

Mrs. Dazzle. And for Mary—dear! dear!
where fhall we get a Mary?

Mifs. Tell you—all in way of rehearfal—young
lady you juft lock'd in—fhe's in fame fituation you
know.

Mrs. Dazzle. So fhe is—here, Worry!—here's
an excellent opportunity to take her to Mr. Alltrade. (*Afide to* Worry, *who nods to her fignificant-
ly.*)—I declare I ca'nt help laughing.

Mifs. No more can I:—Oh damme, I fee it will
produce an effect now?—give me the key (Mrs.
Dazzle *gives it him*).—All to our feparate places,
and let rehearfal begin.—Enter Duke of Norfolk.
(*Puts himfelf in a mock tragic attitude, and fpeaks
bombaftically.*) "Now! by my holy dame, with
" this fame key, Jockey of Norfolk, thou'lt unlock
" the gate of Scottifh Mary's prifon. (*Unlocks
" folding doors, and leads out* Juliana).—Befhrew
" me, but you're fafe, and fo good morrow, good
" Queen Elizabeth!"

Mrs. Dazzle (*alfo fpeaking bombaftically*).
" Go to—we'll nip 'em in the bud.—Why, how
" now, rebels?—For this treacherous Queen—
" (*feizing* Juliana, *and delivering her to* Worry;
" who puts himfelf in a tragic attitude)—convey
" her to the tower!—and there, good Burleigh
" —You take the hint!—Away!"   *Mifs,*

Miſt. Ay :—You take the hint !—Away !

Worry. Oh yes :—I take the hint—Away ! (*Exit with* JULIANA).

Mrs. Dazzle. Bravo !—will it meet with diſapprobation now ?—

Miſt. No—it muſt be a very illnatured audience indeed, that don't applaud ſo ingenious an exit.—

Mrs. Dazzle. Ay: there's authorſhip for you !

Miſt. Egad, and there's management for you !

Mrs. Dazzle. Remember, Sir, but for me theſe characters wouldn't have been brought on the ſtage.

Miſt. No ; and but for you they wouldn't have been got off the ſtage ; but now to get Norfolk off——Muſt follow new actreſs.—(*Aſide.*)

Mrs. Dazzle. Stop ! I'll tell you ; Elizabeth firſt turns her back upon him—then Norfolk makes a long harangue—then——

Miſt. Pſha ! hang long harangues,—touch and go,—that's the plan for effect ; I'll ſhew you how to do Norfolk's exit !—firſt turn your back on me P. S.—(Mrs. DAZZLE *turns her back on him.*)— So, then I ſtrut off O. P.—Gently—don't turn round till I'm gone : then work yourſelf into a furious paſſion.—Mary, I fly !—I follow thee ! and ſo, good morrow, good Queen Elizabeth !—— Hem,—there's another good exit ! [*Exit.*

Mrs. Dazzle. Oh, the old fool ! how I ſhall wheedle him !

Enter Sir HERVEY *and* ALLTRADE.

Sir Hervey. Madam !

Mrs. Dazzle. Is he gone ! now then to work my-ſelf into a furious paſſion—(*turns round.*)—thou wretch ! thou traitor !—How ! Sir Hervey !—Mr. ——Heavens ! have you ſeen nothing of Miſs Sutherland ?—(*to* ALLTRADE.)

Alltrade.

Alltrade. No; and Sir Hervey has brought the bond on purpofe for me to prefent to her, and now, to our aftonifhment, we find fhe and Worry have juft gone out of the caftle together:—what can it mean?

Mrs. Dazzle. Mean! *(burfts into tears)*—that I am wheedl'd myfelf.—Oh that brute of a manager!—Sir Hervey, 'tis too plain—fhe has elop'd.—

Sir Hervey. Elop'd!

Mrs. Dazzle. No doubt fhe has fled to Captain Lavifh; and thefe two impoftors are his agents.—oh, I fee it all! fhe has long intended it; and to avoid figning the bond, fhe has haftened her departure.

Sir Hervey. Elope with Lavifh, why this outdoes her mother:—but can I ftand idly by?—no—I'll difappoint my enemy of this unmanly triumph, and fave her; fpite of herfelf I'll fave her—Mr. Alltrade, wait upon him inftantly, and bid him reftore my daughter on pain of a fecond and more defperate meeting.—Come, madam, we'll fee him on his way.

Mrs. Dazzle. By all means, Sir Hervey: I only hope you don't blame me for my pupil's indifcretion.

Sir Hervey. No: had fhe copied your bright and excellent example, this ne'er had happened—but though her errors even exceed her mother's, and a reconciliation is more than ever diftant, yet fhe is ftill my child!—and in a moment dangerous as the prefent, for my own fake I'll prove a friend and father. [*Exeunt.*

THE END OF THE SECOND ACT.

ACT III.

SCENE—*An Apartment in* Lavish's *House—
Recefs with fmall Folding Doors, which are
thrown open, and difcover a Marble Pedeftal
furrounded by Doves and Cupids—a Table with
Wine and Refrefhments upon it.*

Enter Frank *and a* Workman.

Frank. Ha! ha! fo you've no fooner finifh-
ed that whimfical out-of-the-way job (*pointing
to the recefs*)—than he fends for you about
another.

Workman. Ay, your mafter is an excellent cuf-
tomer,—always up to his chin in brick and mor-
tar; and then for price—'gad! he never haggles
about price.

Frank. No, and the beft of the joke is, he calls
himfelf an economift, and comes down here on a
faving fcheme.

Workman. A faving fcheme!

Frank. Ay! finding himfelf a little out of elbows
in London, and the prefent ftate of the Continent
not allowing him to travel, he came here to
live

live cheap, and retrench.—And there! (*pointing to recefs again*)—there's one fpecimen of his economy.—On the journey he bought a ftatue of Venus.

Workman. I know; and a great bargain it was: it only coft him five pounds.

Frank. True; but not choofing to have his beauties gazed at, he employed you to build that ftrange fort of recefs to put it in, which has coft him at leaft five times the fum.—This is always the way; if he bought a cheap boat, he'd cut a canal for it; and if a pulpit, he'd build a church for it:—in fact, he is a falfe economift—a felf-deceiver; and here he comes to elucidate my defcription.

Enter LAVISH.

Lavifh. Oh! if I go on in this clofe faving way only fix months longer, I fhall be able to return to town and dafh like the beft of them:—never was fuch a hand at buying bargains.—Frank, come here you rogue:—juft now, at Squire Brozier's fale, what do you think I gave for a curricle? — only forty pounds!—there, there's economy for you.

Frank. Economy!—begging your pardon, Sir,—I fee no economy in buying what you don't want.

Lavifh. How?—would you let a bargain flip through your fingers, you extravagant rafcal?

Frank. No—but you've no horfes, Sir; and a curricle's ufelefs——

Lavifh. That's what I faid: fays I, a curricle is ufelefs without horfes,—fo I bought a pair directly.

Frank. Bought a pair?

Lavifh.

Lavifh. Ay, gave a hundred and twenty pounds for them—to be fure it's money; but one's own carriage faves pofting and drivers: in fhort, the worft come to the worft, 'tis but a hundred and fifty pounds, and I'll fave it a thoufand ways.— Who are you, Sir? *(to Workman.)*

Workman. I have finifh'd that job, all but fixing up the ftatue, Sir; and now I come about the billiard-room:—but, to fpeak honeftly, it is not worth repairing.

Lavifh. So I thought; I thought it wasn't worth repairing.

Workman. No, Sir; and a new room will not coft above three hundred pounds:—but then to be fure it will be elegant and lafting.

Lavifh. So it will, and the firft expence is the leaft; fo up with the new room.—*(Workman exit.)* —And now to finifh my vindication to Juliana— *(Sits at the table and writes)*:—" Your late mo-
" ther was not only my relation, but my friend
" and benefactrefs; and on Sir Hervey's one day
" reprobating her conduct with unufual afperity,
" gratitude prompted me to defend it perhaps
" more warmly than I ought, and a duel was the
" refult."—*(Knocking at the door.)*—See who's there.—(FRANK *exit.*)—But what fignifies writing? while fhe's immured in her prefent den, I haven't a chance of fuccefs.—Mrs. Dazzle formerly feduced me into fome gallantries, and a difappointed widow is the devil.

Re-enter FRANK *laughing.*

Frank. Sir, I beg pardon for laughing; but who do you think is at the door?—no lefs a gentleman

than the one you caned at Newmarket about four
years ago.

Lavifh. Caned!—Oh! I recollect—I detected
him in an act of forgery.—But what does the fellow want?—I don't know his name, nor have I
once feen him fince.

Frank. No; and though he now afks for Captain Lavifh, he little thinks you are the gentleman
he is under fuch obligations to.

Lavifh. Shew him up (FRANK *exit*);—introduce the Newmarket gentleman to his two old
antagonifts the Captain and his cane.—And, in
the mean time—(*Sits at table, and takes up pen
again*).

Enter FRANK *and* ALLTRADE.

Frank. This way, Sir—there, that's my mafter
(*pointing to* LAVISH, *whofe back is turned towards* ALLTRADE).

Alltrade. Oh, that's Captain Lavifh, is it?—
Sir, I wait upon you——

Lavifh (*not regarding him*). Yes, the widow is
fo jealous and fo violent.—(*Turns round.*)—How
d'ye do, my fine fellow?—how d'ye do?——My
Newmarket hero fure enough.—(*Afide.*)

Alltrade (*trembling*). Amazement! why it's the
very man who——

Lavifh. What's the matter?—you feem cold—
fhall I warm you?

Alltrade. Warm me!—no—I——

Lavifh. Some wine—give the gentleman fome
wine.—This is the houfe of frugality, and therefore
I can't offer you a great variety; but as far as
Burgundy, Madeira, and Champagne—muft drink
them, if I fave it a thoufand ways,

Alltrade.

Alltrade. Sir, you'll excufe me.——Why furely I've miftaken my man—he would never be fo civil: at all events he don't recollect me ; fo I'll pluck up courage.—(*Afide.*)——Sir, I wait upon you from Sir Hervey Sutherland : he arrived here to-day, and knowing of your love for his daugh-ter——

Lavifh. Came down to increafe her confine-ment, I fuppofe.

Alltrade. No trifling, Sir ; he is convinced you are concerned in her elopement——

Lavifh. Elopement !—how !—what !—Juliana eloped ?

Alltrade. You know fhe has, Sir ; and Sir Her-vey infifts——

Lavifh. Eloped !—Juliana free !—out of the widow's and her father's cuftody !—Which way did fhe go ?—what road did fhe take ?—fpeak, fpeak this inftant.

Alltrade. I fpeak !—if I knew, of courfe you would be the laft man I fhould give information to.

Lavifh. Indeed !

Alltrade. Certainly.—Sir Hervey is my friend, and if his daughter isn't at prefent in your power, I fhall unite with him in oppofing your purfuit of her.

Lavifh. You will !

Alltrade. Undoubtedly.

Lavifh. Pray, Sir, were you ever at New-market ?

Alltrade. Newmarket, Sir !—I—I——

Lavifh. Ay, Newmarket, Sir, Newmarket.—Frank, give me my cane.

Alltrade. Stay, Sir—what do you want with your cane ?

Lavifh

Lavish (taking cane from FRANK). Only to help
your memory.—Look!—*(shaking it)*—were you
ever at Newmarket?

Alltrade (bowing). Yes, I was, Sir.

Lavish. And you'll oppofe me in purfuing——

Alltrade. No, believe me, Sir.

Lavish. And if you knew which road fhe took—

Alltrade. I'd tell you, upon my honour, Sir.

Lavish. Then retire—begone this inftant.——
And d'ye hear, if you're not fatisfied with this treat-
ment, call again, and I'll give you a warmer reception—*(shaking his cane,* ALLTRADE *exit*).——,
And now for Juliana—now for the idol of my foul!
—Frank, get the curricle: no, I fhall only hurry
and lame my own horfes—get a chaife and four.

Frank. Chaife and four!—is this the way to retrench?—and confider, Sir, Mifs Sutherland has
no money; and you always faid you'd never marry
any woman who had lefs than ten thoufand pounds.

Lavish. I did: but that's an aukward fum: a
woman with ten thoufand pounds expects houfes,
horfes, carriages—in fhort, to fpend double her own
income, and her hufband's too. But a woman
without a farthing; fhe manages the houfe, mends
the linen, nurfes the children, fcolds the fervants—
Oh! that's the real rich wife—and the poor Juliana will be the beft bargain I ever made.—So go,
do as I tell you: and obferve, I'll marry her if I
facrifice my whole fortune in the purfuit.

Frank. Sacrifice your whole fortune, Sir!

Lavish. Ay, I will, if I fave it a thoufand ways.

[*Exeunt.*

SCENE—*Outſide of* LAVISH's *Houſe.*

Enter Mrs. DAZZLE—*her hat and cloak on.*

Mrs. Dazzle. So, now to enter this perfidious Captain's houſe.—Not only love and jealouſy urge me to ſeparate him and Juliana; but as I know he don't mean to marry her, it is my buſineſs to get her once more into Alltrade's power:—yes, Miſs Juliana; let me recover my huſband's hundred thouſand pounds, and I'll warrant I'll recover my Captain. He, like the reſt of the world, won't viſit virtue in a cottage, but place me in a magnificent houſe,—ay, there's the ſecret:—now-a-days people viſit the building, not the owner of it; and on the ſize of the rooms, and the number of the entertainments, we may not only calculate our friends and admirers, but alſo the good and bad opinion of the whole faſhionable world!

[*Exit into* LAVISH's *houſe.*

Enter WORRY *and* JULIANA.

Juliana. Look out; we are purſued:—I'm ſure they were Mrs. Dazzle's ſervants.

Worry. They were! but we've outrun them.

Juliana. Yes: but if they come up with us, I ſhall be forced back and endure encreaſed perſecution:—Oh! I wiſh we were ſafe at this Mr. MIST's houſe.

Worry. So do I:—though you ſee what a ſtrange gentleman he is!—he left us to examine the firſt flow waggon we met; but don't deſpond, madam:—I won't leave you—no, I'll die firſt.

D 3 *Juliana.*

Juliana. Kind—generous ! but I cannot bear to involve you : remember you have a wife, and—

Worry. Remember !—I fhall never forget it !

Juliana. Nay : but a hufband is of fo much confequence to his family—

Worry. Blefs you, I'm of no confequence ; nobody ever wants me :—if any body leaves a card, it's for Mrs. Worry :—if any body fends an invitation, it's for Mrs. Worry :—if an invitation is fent in return, it's ftill Mrs. Worry : nobody calls or afks after the hufband, except indeed the tradefpeople !—they are kind enough now and then to notice me : but like other great married men, I'm obliged to be out when they call: fo, curfe me if I've even the pleafure of being at home to a dun ! but we wafte time, let us proceed to Mr. Mift's houfe.

Juliana. Ay : for Heaven's fake difpatch—

Alltrade (without). You take that fide of the road, I'll take this :—fhe cannot efcape then.

Juliana. There, 'tis Mr. Alltrade's voice !— and both fides of the road are guarded by enemies.

Worry. Yes: it's all over—we're between two fires.—Which way fhall we go ?—(*Pointing to* LAVISH's *door:*) that door ftands moft invitingly open, fuppofe we enter it.

Juliana. Do—inftantly: why, what's the matter? you were quite valiant juft now !

Worry. I was : but I fancy my courage is more like a new acquaintance than an old friend,—profeffes a great deal at firft, but generally fneaks off in the hour of danger : however, lead on—and let us hope to receive from ftrangers that protection which friends have denied us.

[*Exeunt into* LAVISH's *houfe.*

Enter

Enter ALLTRADE.

Alltrade. So—there fhe goes into Captain LA-
VISH's houfe : bravo, Mifs JULIANA!—and there
fhe may ftay for me: I'll to Sir Hervey inftantly,
and let him come himfelf and fight it out: for all
the legacies regiftered in Doctors Commons fhould
not induce me to re-enter thofe doors and receive
another warm reception!   [*Exit.*

SCENE—*Infide* LAVISH's *houfe, recefs, &c. as in
firft Scene of this Act.*

Enter LAVISH *and* Mrs. DAZZLE.

Lavifh. Now you've fearched every part of the
houfe; now are you fatisfied Mifs Sutherland is
not concealed in it?—'Sdeath! to detain me at
fuch a moment—(*Afide*).
Mrs. Dazzle. No:—fhe's not in the houfe I grant
you; but the chaife! the chaife and four!—pray,
moft economical Captain, do you ufually travel with
four horfes?
Lavifh. Always:—it's by far the cheapeft plan:
it fhortens the journey, faves ftopping at inns; in
fhort, the additional fhilling is no object, and if I
had but ten pounds a-year, I'd always travel with
four horfes:—and now, my dear widow, allow me
to fee you home.
Mrs. Dazzle. Take care, Sir:—difappointed love
knows no bounds; and recollect it is in my power to
expofe you to my rival:—I have your letters in my
poffeffion,—letters in which you laugh and rail at
marriage:—letters—
Lavifh.

Lavifh. Nay, be patient.—There now! this it is to be dragooned into an attachment,—fhe has me, by all that's frugal!—(*Afide.*)—Come then, fit down, and let us drink to the revival of our friend-fhip!—See: here's famous Madeira!—ay: you may ftare: but this too is on the cheapeft plan I promife you, for while it takes two bottles of port to make me drunk, one of Madeira does it completely.—So here's to the rival—(*tapping hard at ftage door P. S.*)—Why, what's that? ha!

Mrs. Dazzle. Mercy!—fomebody's coming!—for heaven's fake don't let me be feen—I'll ftep into this room—(*Goes to ftage door O. P. and tapping heard there*).

Worry (*outfide the door*). Madam, where are you, madam?

Mrs. Dazzle. Why, what is all this?—it is done on purpofe to expofe me!—Oh, Mr. Lavifh! if you have either feeling or gallantry, think of my fitua-tion: a widow only a fortnight, and to be detected alone in a Captain's houfe!—

Lavifh. Well! ftep into that recefs—quick, quick—(Mrs. DAZZLE *in her hurry drops her cloak, then enters recefs, and* LAVISH *faftens the door upon her*).—So—there I have you faft; and now— (*taking his cane from the table*).

Juliana (*outfide the door P. S*). Mr. Worry, why don't you anfwer? me, my dear Mr. Worry.

Lavifh. Damme, I'll Worry you—I'll anfwer you (*opens door and enter* JULIANA): Heaven's! Mifs Sutherland!

Juliana. Mr. Lavifh! I beg pardon, Sir:—when I took refuge in this houfe, I little thought to meet you.—Good day, Sir. (*Going*).

Lavifh. What! now—the very moment that I've found you?

Juliana,

Juliana. What can I do, Mr. Lavifh!—I own I owe you obligations—nay, more—I confefs I could have loved you :—but I have told you my determination—you are my father's enemy—therefore we cannot be friends :—farewel, Sir!

Lavifh. Mighty well, madam, mighty well!— but this isn't your real motive—you love another : you love this Mr. Worry!—anfwer me candidly, ma'am!—did he not run away with you ?

Juliana. He did!—but——

Lavifh. He did!—then may I run into every fpecies of extravagance, if when I catch him, I don't give him the Newmarket flourifh *(fhaking his cane)*.—Where is he ? — where is this Mr. Worry ?

Enter WORRY.

Worry. Here at your fervice, Sir.

Lavifh. This my rival!—this antient, wizen, dowager-like—Don't be unmanly, Lavifh!—never ftrike an old woman 1 intreat you *(throwing away his cane)*.—Befides now I look at him, it is! 'tis Sir Hervey's—you dear, amiable, agreeable :—one Mrs. WORRY is fufficient for you, or the devil's in't.

Worry. Very likely, Sir : but if you have no rival in an old woman, as you pleafe to call me, I fancy Mifs Sutherland has ! when 1 liftened at the door, I'll fwear I heard the widow's voice.

Lavifh. The widow!—no, Juliana—I can prove myfelf as great an economift in love as in money.

Worry. Are you fure you can, Sir ?

Lavifh. Sure!—if fince the hour I firft beheld her, I haven't treafured every thought, hoarded every look !—ftored——

Worry

Worry (*pointing to Mrs.* DAZZLE'*s cloak on the* ground). Pray, Sir, who does that cloak belong to?

Lavish. That cloak!——Oh that cloak is one of my bargains.

Worry. Is it? then you buy very dear bargains, I fancy.—Look, madam,—(*taking up cloak*) isn't it Mrs. Dazzle's?

Juliana. It is: and since this confirms what I have long suspected, I have now an additional motive for avoiding you.—Mr. Lavish, we never meet again.—Come (*to* WORRY)!

Worry (*to* LAVISH). I say, if you don't hoard your money better than your love, never think of matrimony—you'll find it too expensive a bargain for you, I promise you. (*Going.*)

Sir Hervey Sutherland (*without*). Where is he? —where is Captain Lavish?

Lavish. Sir Hervey! 'Slife! what brings him here?

Juliana. My father! oh Heavens! and to find me under the roof of his enemy——

Worry. And me also!—Mrs. Worry herself couldn't terrify me more.—Come along, madam, and let's leave the Captain to stand the brunt.—

Juliana. Ay: lose not a moment.—And oh, Mr. Lavish! as this is the last time we shall ever meet, remember the parting words of her you once regarded—Pacify my father, do not incence him—be his friend, and 'spite of your falshood and unkindness, you may still be mine.

Worry. And mine—ha! ha! there's another bad bargain for him!

(JULIANA *exit*—WORRY *is following, when* LAVISH *lays hold of him and prevents his going*). Holloa! what's the matter?

Enter

Enter Sir HERVEY.

Sir Hervey. So, Mr. Lavifh; 'tis ftill doomed that we're to meet as enemies—where is Mifs Sutherland, Sir?

Lavifh. Sir Hervey, on the honour of a gentleman, I know nothing of your daughter's elopement; for any further information I refer you to Mr. Worry (*pufhing* WORRY *forwards*). I fay, who has the belt of the bargain now?

Sir Hervey. 'Sdeath! I've a great mind—(*advancing towards* WORRY, *and ftopping*)—but he is only agent;—to you as principal, I look for reparation and redrefs.—Hear mé, Sir—Mrs. Dazzle, a lady of the ftricteft truth and honour—fhe firft informed me of your infamous defigns, and now— not half an hour ago, a friend, on whofe word I can equally rely, faw Mifs Sutherland enter this very houfe : therefore there is no alternative but this— inftantly reftore her, or——you guefs the refult.

Lavifh. I do—but I'll wafte no more powder, Sir Hervey.

Sir Hervey. How?

Lavifh. No : dying is certainly a cheap mode of living, and to a man in defperate circumftances, a duel may be a good faving fcheme : but having hoarded enough to make life comfortable, why I'm a curft fool if I don't fave it a thoufand ways. (*Sits down*).

Sir Hervey. Poor, paltry prevarication!—Remember, Mr. Lavifh, we were once friends—I treated you as a fon—you efteemed me as a parent—and what diffolved that friendfhip?—you chofe to vindicate the honour of a falfe wife, and call me to the field—did I not come?

Lavifh. You did, Sir.

Sir

Sir Hervey. And now where is your confiftency?
—you would bring my daughter to the fame degraded ftate; you would reduce her to the level of
her mother; and when an injured father afks for
fatisfaction, you refufe to give it him—what is this
but cowardice? plain unequivocal cowardice!

Lavifh. Cowardice! ill as Mifs Sutherland has
treated me, I never meant to raife my arm againft
her father:—but when you allude to the memory
of her I owe fuch obligations to, and fay I would
reduce her daughter to the fame degraded ftate—
'tis paft bearing—I can't endure it! and you may
fhoot me as foon as you pleafe.

Sir Hervey. Here are the weapons then—*(putting piftol into* LAVISH'*s hand).*

Worry. Hold, Sir; he is innocent, Mifs Sutherland is flandered!—the lady your friend faw enter
this houfe was a very different perfon—it was the
widow, indeed it was the widow!

Sir Hervey. Mrs. Dazzle?

Worry. Ay: 'tis fhe that carries on an amour
with the Captain; and though I can't produce her
to prove it, I can at leaft produce a part of her;—
look, Sir—do you fee this cloak?

Sir Hervey. Away! 'tis my unfeeling daughter's,
and the fight fo heightens my refentment——
Come, Sir, wrongs like mine will brook no more
delay, and you muft either meet a coward's or a
villain's fate——

Lavifh. Coward again!—Come, then—here's
my ground! *(goes up ftage.)*

Worry (ftopping Sir HERVEY). Don't think me
impertinent Sir—but while you as a man of honour
think it your duty to fight a duel, I as an honeft
man think it mine to prevent it!—it's the widow!

upon

upon ' my foul, it's the widow ! (*holding* Sir
Hervey's *arm who ſtruggles to get it looſened.*)

Sir Hervey. Diſtraction !—nay then—thus——
(*throws* Worry *violently from him, who, falling
againſt doors of receſs, they burſt open and* Mrs.
Dazzle *is diſcovered ſtanding on the pedeſtal ſur-
rounded by doves, &c.*)

Worry (*who has fallen at her feet, ſtill looking up
in her face*). It's the widow !—upon my foul it's
the widow !

Sir Hervey. Amazement !—can that be Mrs.
Dazzle !

Laviſh. No—it's a ſtatue—you fee it's a ſtatue.

(*Mrs.* Dazzle *riſes, walks quickly down the ſtage
and exit.*)

Worry. Halloa ! won't you take your cloak
along with you ? you'll want it to cover your fins !

Sir Hervey. Hypocrite ! I now view her in her
true colours, and I am doomed to be the dupe of
woman.—Mr. Laviſh, I fee my friend was miſtaken,
and I acknowledge I have wronged you.

Laviſh. Pſha !—I want no acknowledgment—
if you wiſh to make me amends, ſtay and dine
with me—mine is the ſyſtem of economy, and as I
can't lay out money to better advantage than in
entertaining an old friend, I'll give you a dinner
fit for the court of Aldermen—I will, if I ſave it a
thouſand ways.

Sir Hervey. Excuſe me, Sir—your innocence on
the preſent occaſion will not do away former injuries ; nor will Mrs. Dazzle's bad conduct be an
apology for my daughter's.— No !—whilſt I thought
love the cauſe of her elopement, it was my duty to
purſue and ſave her :—but ſince I fee felf-intereſt is
the motive, and that ſhe fled to avoid ſigning an
inſtrument which would have ſaved me from diſgrace,

grace, and not have injured her—I fhall no longer condefcend to feek her.

Worry. 'Tis no fuch thing, Sir—and if you will go to her at Mr. Mift's houfe—

Sir Hervey. Peace!—and inftantly attend me home, where, if the account of your own conduct prove not fatisfactory—(WORRY *attempts to fpeak*). —Nay, this is no place for explanation—go on be- fore—Mr. Lavifh,· I have the honour to wifh you good evening! (WORRY *and Sir* HERVEY *exeunt.*)

Lavifh. Here's bad reckoning!—'tis well I cal- culate better in money matters. But what's to be done?—he faid fhe was gone to Mr. Mift's:—well! if I follow her, fhe won't fee me;—if I write to her, fhe won't anfwer my letter.—Oh! fhe's loft!— Juliana's loft to me for ever!

Enter FRANK.

Frank. Sir, is the chaife to wait?

Lavifh (*not regarding him*). And yet,—if I could gain an interview——hark'ye, Frank—do you know any body at Mr. Mift's the Manager's?

Frank. Yes: and fo do you, Sir—Stopgap, who left your fervice to go on the ftage, is now his prompter.

Lavifh. That's fortunate—I'll go to him in- ftantly; and if he will but do me a favour—

Frank. That he will, if you'll bribe him: only give him ten pounds——but that you know, Sir, won't fuit your fyftem of economy.

Lavifh. Won't it?—ten pound is no object, and I've lately made fo many good bargains, that it's d——d hard if I can't afford to throw away an odd bank note or two.—So, come along—and if after all I do live a little beyond my income, it's no fault of mine, Frank.

Frank,

Frank. No! whofe is it then, Sir?

Lavifh. Whofe!—why it is the fault of thofe felfifh harpies who make economy ufelefs—who raife the price of every article:—and if Sir Hervey and other fighting gentlemen would unload their piftols on jobbers, foreftallers, and monopolizers, their valour would be directed to the beft purpofes— I might live cheap, and the country would be cleared of it's worft enemies! [*Exeunt.*

THE END OF THE THIRD ACT.

ACT IV.

SCENE—*Outſide of a Theatre, and* MIST's *houſe;* LAVISH *diſcovered liſtening at the door.*

Laviſh. Gad! I hope the prompter don't want prompting: (*Looking at his watch*) By this 'tis ten minutes, but by my reckoning ten hours, ſince Stopgap entered this houſe with a letter for Juliana, —ſo—he comes!—he comes!

Enter STOPGAP (*from the houſe*).

Laviſh. Well! what news?—have you ſeen Miſs Sutherland?

Stopgap. I have, and here—(*producing a letter*).

Laviſh. Here's an anſwer to my letter.

Stopgap. No;—there's your letter back again— ſhe refuſed to open it, and in my preſence ordered the ſervants not to admit you into the houſe.

Laviſh. What! ſhe perſiſts——

Stopgap. Moſt obſtinately, Sir;—but ſpite of her refuſal, make it worth my while, and I'll procure you an interview:—excuſe the hint, Sir; but if you recollect when I lived with you, you were ſo ſaving——

Laviſh. So I am ſtill:—worſe and worſe,—more economical than ever;—but the hope of gaining ſuch a treaſure as Juliana!—here you rogue,— here's ten pounds on the ſtrength of it (*giving him a bank note*).

Stopgap.

Stopgap. So there is ;—then liften :—the play to
night is the " Road to Ruin," and Mr. Prettyman,
who was to have performed Goldfinch, has juft met
with an accident :—now, Sir, having no fubftitute,
and it being too late to change the play, fuppofe
you wait on the Manager, and offer to fupply his
place.

Lavifh. I fupply !

Stopgap. Why not ? at the private theatre I have
feen you act this very part :—then an interview is
certain ; for Mr. Mift's houfe adjoins the theatre,
and Mifs Sutherland is now in a room clofe to the
ftage.

Lavifh. Is fhe ?—then I'll double Prettyman ;
—I'll act Goldfinch,—" that's your fort;"—but
hold, hold—don't introduce me by my own name;
call me Mr. Crib, or Mr. Glib, or Mr. Squib.

Stopgap. I will ; I'll call you Mr. Squib.—Hufh !
—he comes. (*They ftand afide.*)

Enter MIST *and* Mrs. DAZZLE.

Mift. How! what! London Manager !—Hufband
die a London Manager !—Go on, imperial Mrs.
M. P.

Mrs. Dazzle. Nay, I only tell you that Mr.
Dazzle, a fhort time previous to his deceafe, was in
treaty for a moiety of one of the London theatres ;
but I cannot fay whether he lived to complete his
purchafe ;—however, I fhall write by this poft.

Mift. And fo will I :—and if he did purchafe,
throne devolves to you.—Blefs me ! how majeftic
fhe looks !—and her play.—When fhall I hear the
reft of your moft magnificent play ?—Nay, fpare a
country monarch :—thought her great actrefs,—

you humble author!—now you turn out manager,
and she worse than a dummy.

Mrs. Dazzle. Well, Sir, you know how to
make atonement; your friend Mr. Alltrade wishes
to marry this ungrateful girl, and as she is now
under your roof——

Mist. Enough—send for Alltrade, and then,
" Good morrow, good Queen Mary."

Mrs. Dazzle. I will;—I'll go write to him instantly;—and in return, if I do possess a London
theatre, depend on't you shall be my sole manager.

Mist. Right!—I'm the man to rule behind
curtain.—I'm the man to accept pieces, cast parts,
and every night secure an overflow;—but go, thou
author of the divinest tragedy (*kisses her hand, and
Mrs.* DAZZLE *it*). Never shall it be acted though;
never shall she act her own infernal——

Stopgap (advancing). Sir!—more bad luck,
Sir!—Mr. Prettyman, in trying to pull on the only
pair of new boots we have in the theatre, has just
put out his shoulder bone, consequently there is
nobody to act Goldfinch.

Mist. Put out shoulder bone!—what now!—
Just before doors open?

Stopgap. Even so, Sir; and we have lately
made so many apologies——

Mist. True; made one last night, two the
night before: zounds! there'll be a riot; and all
owing to this ungrateful shamming——See how it
is—benefit's over—that's it—got four pounds
over expences, and till that's gone, act Road to
Ruin off, instead of on, the stage; but what's to
be done?—found out, Stop; d——e we shall be
found out.

Stopgap.

Stopgap. Nay: there is hope ſtill—look yonder, Sir; that gentleman is an excellent ſubſtitute; he is perfeƈt in the part, and with your leave is ready to go on with it.—I'll introduce him—Mr. Squib, this is Mr. Miſt.

Laviſh. Sir, your moſt devoted——

Miſt (haughtily). Servant, my lad; ſervant—ſo, call yourſelf an aƈtor! heh! hem!

Laviſh. I do—at your ſervice, Sir.

Miſt. My ſervice!—he! he!—that's another matter—ſee you aƈt firſt—if miſs, exit Squib—if hit, enter at half a guinea a week.

Laviſh. Pſha!—money's no objeƈt.

Miſt. No!

Laviſh. No, I've ſaved a fortune, Mr. Manager, and am ſo attached to the ſtage, that I'll not only aƈt gratis, but when there are not expences in the houſe, I'll be bound to pay them—I will, if I ſave it a thouſand ways.

Miſt. Will you?—oh that I had a whole company like him!—why you're a high fellow!

Laviſh (ſpeaking from GOLDFINCH.) "To be "ſure—know the odds—hold four in hand—beat "the mail—come in full ſpeed—rattle down the "gateway—take care of your heads—never killed "but one woman and a child in all my life—that's "your fort!"

Miſt. Bravo!—capital!—and no ſalary!—my dear Mr. Squib—all gratitude—all thankfulneſs—by and bye rule a London theatre—perhaps·Covent Garden—Know preſent aƈting manager!

Laviſh. What!

Miſt. Mum!—kick him out, whip you in.

Laviſh. That's right—kick out preſent ſtupid aƈting manager, and whip me in;—but come along —isn't it time to dreſs?

Mift. Not quite; juft time to crack bottle, and draw up apology—muft get one ready written:—much warfare lately—laft night affronted audience myfelf.

Lavifh. Yourfelf! how?

Mift. Tell you:—whenever theatre's thin, always get drunk.

Lavifh. In the name of heaven, why?

Mift. He! he! he!—'caufe it makes me fee double—fo going to take a peep, miftook my way, and in dagger fcene of Macbeth, reeled upon the ftage, and ftaggered up to lamps!—never fo well received before;—delighted with applaufe, ftood fmiling and bowing, till Macbeth bore me off, 'midft the fhouting and huzzaing of a genteel, though not a numerous, audience—Expect buftle to night in confequence—fo muft knock under a little —not too much though—I'm Manager—heh!— hem!—but come along; and over bottle drink fuccefs——

Lavifh. There's no occafion; my Goldfinch never failed—" that's your fort!" [*Exeunt.*

SCENE—*A grand Saloon in Sutherland Houfe —Mafks difcovered dancing.*

After dance, ALLTRADE *dreffed in a Domino enters with a Servant.*

Alltrade (a letter in his hand). From Mrs. Dazzle, you fay; perhaps fome news of Mifs Sutherland. *(Opens letter and reads)*: " *Juliana* " is at Mr. Mift's, and he completely in our in- " tereft.—Come directly, and if Sir Hervey has " given you his confent, make him write it to
" his

" his daughter: and if he objects to that from
" motives of pride and delicacy, bid him write to
" the Manager, and entreat him to enforce his
" command: this shewn to Juliana will secure all;
" —she will forfeit the legacy, and a third of my
" husband's estate will be yours!"————Excellent! and he has given me his consent—what's
here? a postscript!—*(Reads on)*: " If Juliana has
" signed the bond, don't mention it to Sir Hervey
" —he'll expect money, and at present you know
" we have none to give him."————True: and
the bond is already disposed of; for if all else fail,
that will be a grand resource.—My compliments
to Mrs. Dazzle, and I'll wait upon her presently.
(Servant exit.)

Enter Sir HERVEY *hastily.*

Sir Hervey. Alltrade! my friend!—I'm glad
I've found you—*(taking his hand)*.
Alltrade. Why, what agitates you?
Sir Hervey. I'm ruined—I'm exposed—look—
do you see those masks? *(pointing to two masks in
dominos who stand apart from the rest)*.
Alltrade. I do—what of them?
Sir Hervey (whispering him). Hush.
Alltrade. Bailiffs!
Sir Hervey. Ay, an execution for a thousand
pounds, and a writ against my person for nearly
the same sum.—And now, in the meridian of my
splendor, I am to meet the scorn of all around
me; now, in the midst of friends——but be it so—
a gaol can't yield me less substantial joy than this
unmeaning, artificial scene.
Alltrade. Come, come, don't rail at that which,
till now, gave you happiness.

Sir

Sir Hervey. Never.—What has it afforded me? days of diftrefs, and nights of fever and difgrace: borrowing one day, to pay double the next; flying to the gaming-table—facrificing fortune, health, honour—and for what?—to appear fafhionable; to make a falfe difplay of wealth; and fritter away life in the fociety of knaves I deteft, and fools I defpife.—Call you this happinefs?—No, 'tis defperation, 'tis delirium!

Alltrade. Nay, be compofed; there is ftill a way to fave you. You know this diftrefs would have been avoided had your daughter figned the bond.

Sir Hervey Name her not——I do not wifh to curfe her.

Alltrade. Well, but if fhe will ftill fign——and remember our converfation this morning—on your wifhing fhe had a hufband to protect her, and my naming myfelf, you were pleafed to fay fhe could not be in better hands.

Sir Hervey. I did—but what has this to do with——

Alltrade. Every thing.—Let the marriage take place, and I, in the character of hufband, can execute the bond myfelf. Then thefe debts will be difcharged, and all go well again. Come, though you fay you don't diflike a prifon, I am too much your friend to fee you put to the trial.

Sir Hervey. Well, I own I dread the expofure and difgrace.

Alltrade. Then to avoid it, write a ftrong letter to your daughter; ftate that her accepting my hand can alone fave you from ruin.

Sir Hervey I write!—I condefcend!

Alltrade. Nay then, to make it lefs irkfome to your feelings, write to the gentleman under whofe
protection

protection she has placed herself; bid him exert his influence.—Come, step with me into the next room, and I'll dictate the contents.

Sir Hervey. Well, do with me what you will; but I've but little hope.

Alltrade. And I'm most sanguine; and before to-night is past, you shall again enjoy this scene of splendid revelry.

Sir Hervey. What, when I view it in its proper light?—No, my friend; strip dissipation of its robe of fashion—shew it in its naked deformity—see it surrounded by its offspring, poverty, suicide, despair, and madness!—and who would be weak enough to pursue it?—But lead on, I obey your wishes.   [*Exeunt.*

(*Dancing renewed.*)

Re-enter Sir Hervey.

Sir Hervey. So, I have sent the letter.—I know not why, I trembled as I wrote it; and at the thought of thus disposing of my child, my foreboding heart——but I dare think no more—let the dance go on.

Enter Worry.

Worry. Oh, Sir!—such news!—didn't you say Miss Sutherland hadn't signed the bond?

Sir Hervey. I did: and but now my friend Alltrade——

Worry. Your friend!—only listen, Sir—my nephew, I'm sorry to mention it, is an attorney; and he had the impudence to call here and ask for a ticket for your masked ball. Says he, " I can

" support

" fupport a character."—Says I, " That's impof-
" fible, becaufe you've no character to fupport."—
" Nay," fays he, " I'm grown honeft fince I faw
" you."—" Oh! you are, are you?" fays I;
" then pray walk up; novelty at a mafquerade is
" every thing."

Sir Hervey. Pfha! what's this to me?

Worry. You fhall hear, Sir. I am more forry
to mention he is Mr. Alltrade's attorney; and, by
his orders, has juft taken the bond to Mifs Sutherland, at Mr. Mift's.

Sir Hervey. Indeed! and what was the refult?

Worry. What! why the moment he fhewed her
your name at the bottom of it, fhe burft into tears;
then taking up the pen, fhe exclaimed, " Though
" my father is unmindful of my diftreffes, I can
" never forget his; and were it to doom me to
" imprifonment or death, I would execute with
" pleafure."

Sir Hervey. How! and did fhe——

Worry. She did.—And another thing—you
muft have figned the bond without reading it: inftead of two years, 'tis payable on demand.

Sir Hervey. 'Tis falfe! I'll not believe a word.

Worry. I thought fo—I thought this would be the
cafe; and therefore I perfuaded my nephew to
truft me with it—(*produces bond*).—Look, here is
at once a proof of your friend's villainy and your
daughter's virtue!—See how you have wronged
her, and how he has wronged you. But the widow, fhe is the arch agent! and talk of gentlemen
of the long robe, curfe me but I believe there's
more mifchief under one gown than another!

Sir Hervey (*reading bond*). " Juliana Suther-
" land!"—(*weeps and lets bond fall.*)—Where is
fhe, where is my daughter?

Worry.

Worry. How!—do you mean——

Sir Hervey. I do; I mean to prove myfelf her father: the bitter fecret long has rankled here, but now I can divulge it: and if a fhattered heart can once more vibrate at the touch of joy, it will be when I clafp my wronged, exalted child!—Come, let us fly!

Worry. Ay, the fafter the better.—I'm fo happy!—If Mrs. Worry were in Heaven, I couldn't be happier!—(*as they are going, Bailiffs in dominos advance*)

Bailiff. Excufe us, Sir Hervey, we cannot part with you; and unlefs the debt is inftantly paid, we muft conduct you to prifon.

Worry. To prifon!

Sir Hervey. Ay; behold my well timed punifh-ment!—Now, on the brink of happinefs, I am to meet the fure reward of defperation and extra-vagance!

Bailiff. Nay, why upbraid yourfelf, Sir Hervey? a man of your rank couldn't live fhabbily.

Sir Hervey. No; but I might have lived honor-ably; I might have lived within my income; that is the barrier no man of true honour ever paffes: and if ftealing on the highway be punifhed with death, why fhould the more refined robber, who defrauds the induftrious tradefman of the hard earnings by which he is to fupport his family, why fhould he efcape?——Oh! let no man boaft the proud name of gentleman, who contracts debts he cannot pay!—But I attend you—lead on—and yet—Diftraction!—William!

Worry. Sir!

Sir Hervey. The worft I had forgotten: you know not half your mafter's weaknefs, half his

4   villany!

villany !—not an hour ago I wrote a letter, and commanded my daughter to marry——

Worry. Whom, Sir ?

Sir Hervey. The worſt, the vileſt of mankind !

Worry. Mr. Alltrade ?

Sir Hervey. Yes ; I, her father, in return for all her fondneſs and affection, commanded her to link herſelf to infamy, diſhonour !—But is it yet too late to ſave her ?—will ſhe not be merciful ?—oh ! will ſhe not diſobey me ?

Worry. No, ſhe's ſo affectionate, that the moment ſhe reads the letter—

Sir Hervey. Ay, but perhaps ſhe has not yet received it.—Go, loſe not a moment ; 'tis directed to the gentleman at whoſe houſe ſhe now reſides.

Worry. I'll go ; I'll do all I can to ſave her : and, in the mean time, pray keep up your ſpirits, Sir : indeed, indeed you deſerve a better fate.

Sir Hervey. No, I deſerve it all !—think what I am, and what I might have been !—now an outcaſt and a beggar, dragged from my home, and plunged into a priſon !—and, but for faſhion and its errors, that houſe had been a heaven !—But my child !— go—be ſwifter than the letter—ſave her from ſeeing what will make her curſe me ; and, whilſt it dooms her to eternal miſery, will be an everlaſting evidence of my diſgrace !　　　　　[*Exeunt.*

SCENE—*An Apartment in* MIST's *Houſe.*

(*Knocking at the door.*)—*Enter* Mrs. DAZZLE.

Mrs. Dazzle. 'Tis he! 'tis Alltrade! now for
it!—now if Sir Hervey has but conſented to the
marriage.—(*Here* LAVISH *opens door in back ſcene,
and is coming out; but ſeeing* Mrs. DAZZLE *ſtops
and liſtens*). Oh, I'm ſo anxious.—(*Enter* ALL-
TRADE.)—Well! what ſucceſs? will the match take
place?—ſhall I inherit my huſband's eſtate?

Alltrade. You will! this letter from Sir Hervey
to Mr. Miſt will explain and ſecure every thing.

Mrs. Dazzle. Let me ſee—(*takes letter and
reads*): " To Mr. Miſt.—Sir, My daughter
" having placed herſelf under your protection, I
" am induced to think you have an influence over
" her, though her father has none ; therefore let
" me entreat you to exert it, by perſuading her to
" accept the hand of my friend Mr. Alltrade, and
" aſſure her that her marriage with that gentleman
" can alone ſave me from ruin, or lead to the re-
" conciliation, ſhe has ſo long pretended to wiſh
" for.—HERVEY SUTHERLAND."

Alltrade. There! ſhe's too dutiful to refuſe.

Mrs. Dazzle. Oh, the thought of ſaving him
from ruin would of itſelf induce her to conſent ;
but the hope of a reconciliation alſo!—delightful!
charming! Go, take the letter to Mr. Miſt, and
bid him come and ſhew it Juliana directly.

Alltrade. I will.

Mrs. Dazzle. And, d'ye hear ; then away to a
parſon : in the mean time I'll get a licence, and
in leſs than half an hour the marriage ſhall take
place in this very room.

Enter

Enter a Servant.

Servant. Madam, here's a Mr. Worry——
Mrs. Dazzle. Don't admit him; remember you
have orders to admit nobody.—(Servant *exit.*)
Away! difpatch, my friend ; and now Mifs Juliana,
I defy you! neither your father nor your lover,
no, not even the economical Captain, can fave his
darling treafure now.   [*Exit.*
Lavifh (advancing). Can't he? he'll try a
thoufand ways though.—'Sdeath! no fooner reconciled to Juliana—no fooner convinced her of my
truth and affection, than I'm to fee her——If fhe
reads the letter ; all's over! for her laft words were,
"I will marry no man, but the one my father
"felects for me."—and now, when his ruin and a
reconciliation depend on her confenting——plague
on't! I could play the fool and weep: yes, I'm
no niggard here! *(putting his hand to his heart)*—
and if I can purchafe her fafety even at the lofs of
my life, I fhall reckon it the beft bargain I ever
made.
Mift (without). Very well, I'll deliver letter—
I'll make widow amends.
Lavifh. Here he comes, and in his poffeffion
what will for ever ruin me and Juliana; nay, alfo
Sir Hervey :—I'm fure he's under fome dreadful
error; and if I can fave his daughter at this moment,
my triumph will be ten times greater than in fighting him ;—yes, that I fhall call honourable fatisfaction. What can I devife?—fee the letter fhe
fhall not! and there is no way to prevent it but
by getting this credulous old manager out of the
room. Let me fee—I have it!—he talked of a riot
in his theatre !—it will do ! it will do !

Enter

Enter Mist *drunk.*

Mist (the letter in his hand). So, here's Sir Hervey's letter; and I'm to shew it Miss Sutherland; and enforce marriage, and——u·u-up! *(Hiccuping):* methinks I see double again—methinks—no—no I'm not on stage now, 'cause hear no applause: drunk or sober, sure to encourage such a promising young actor.

Lavish (observing him). Drunk too !—better and better !

Mist. He ! he ! he !—wonder how Mr. Squib—how Mr. No Salary's going on ?—says he, " I'm a " private actor !"—" Hem," says I, " more private " the better:"—hope they accept him though ; hope they let him double Prettyman ; if not, here's such an apology ! *(pulling out a paper, and putting it back again)*—such a beautiful, witty composition ; but hold :—now to see Miss Sutherland !

Lavish (coming against him). And now to prevent you. *(Aside.)*—Oh, Sir, I was just going for you : the riot is begun,—the whole theatre is in an uproar.

Mist. Devil ! what !—want Prettyman ?

Lavish. No, they want you—Tell you how it was—Stopgap went on, and claimed their usual indulgence—on which a little tiger-faced fellow exclaimed from the pit, " We'll bear it no longer !—" if the Manager will constantly make apologies, " play the best parts, act his own farces, get drunk, " and reel upon the stage, why the theatre is a nui-" sance !"

Mist. A nuisance !

Lavish. Ay: " And either let him come and " account for his conduct, or let us treat it as a nui-" sance :

"fance:—let us pull it down!"—He was ftrongly
fupported, and I left the whole houfe calling
"Manager! Manager!"—fo go—go directly
(*pulling him*).

Mift. I go! I account!—to whom:—to a five
pound houfe!—to a tiger-faced gentleman, and a
dozen more ungrateful, taftelefs fcoundrels—I!

Lavifh. Taftelefs!

Mift. Yes: haven't I done every thing!—turn'd
author, actor, engaged Harlequin, and half ruined
myfelf to pleafe 'em?—and now—look 'ye, Mr.
Squib, here's my apology—(*taking paper out of his
pocket*):—if that will fatisfy 'em, let Stop read it—
if not, and they ftill abufe me as acting manager,
fee how they like me in another character—
acting magiftrate!—Damme! myfelf and two
conftables 'll take the whole houfe!

Lavifh (*looking at the paper in* Mist's *hand*).
By heaven, he has miftaken!—'tis Sir Hervey's
letter! (*afide*).—Yes! that will do: give me
that apology, and I'll anfwer for every body being
fatisfied—nay! there's no time for hefitation—
they abfolutely threatened to make you go down on
your knees.

Mift. His knees!—a Manager on his knees!—
that for 'em! (*fnapping his fingers and turning
away from* Lavish).

Lavifh. Nay; the apology—'tis, 'tis Sir Hervey's
hand! (*afide*).—Give me the apology.

Mift. That for'em! won't—won't condefcend
to let 'em hear even apology now.

Lavifh. No!—'Sdeath: I've marr'd every
thing. (*Afide*).

Mift. No: foon manage London audience, and
not even to them——but they know better—and
were I before 'em at this moment—inftead of

afking

afking for apology—inftead of approving this mean cowardly piece of writing, they'd applaud me for deftroying it—they would!—fo there!—preferved my character both as man and as Manager! (*tears* Sir HERVEY's *letter.*)

Lavifh. You have! and Juliana's preferved and I'm preferved!—(*Enter* Mrs. DAZZLE.)—" Here " am I, widow—been to Hatchet's—befpoke wed-" ding coach—all flafh—damn the expence—that's " your fort."

Mrs. Dazzle. You here, Sir!—Mr. Mift, have you fhewn Mifs Sutherland her father's letter?

Mift. No; and can't ftay to do it now—muft go quell riot—muft talk to tiger-fac'd gentleman—

Mrs. Dazzle (ftopping him). Nay: if you wifh to make me amends, I infift you do it inftantly, and let me be eye witnefs of his mortification and her defpair—Come forth, Mifs Juliana!—(*opens door in back fcene, and leads out* JULIANA).—Now, Mr. Mift, where is Sir Hervey's letter?

Mift. Here (*pulling out paper*).

Mrs. Dazzle. Then read it, and fecure my triumph.

Mift. I will—hem! (*Reads*).—" Ladies and " Gentlemen, the difagreeable dilemma to which I " am reduced——"

Mrs. Dazzle (fnatching it from him). Why, you miftake—let me read.—(*Reads*)—" Ladies " and Gentlemen, the difagreeable dilemma to which " I am reduced——" why what's this paper?

Mift. An apology—that I'm ready to offer you, though not audience—I'm very forry, but can't ftay to explain now—(*Going*).

Mrs. Dazzle. Aftonifhing!—why, what's be-come of Sir Hervey's letter?

Mift.

Mifl. What! (*points to the torn letter*).—You take the hint—muſt go to tiger faced gentleman—you take the hint.   [*Exit.*

Mrs. Dazzle. What can he mean!—I'll follow him, and have the matter explained inſtantly—and don't fancy to efcape, Miſs Juliana; for Sir Hervey ſhall come himſelf and enforce his confent; and if that fails,—the bond—look to the bond—Oh, you may ſmile, Sir (*to* LAVISH), but you'll find revenge is ſtill in my power.   [*Exit.*

Lavifh. You hear, Miſs Sutherland; and to avoid the danger with which you are threatened take my advice and be beforehand with them.— Fly to your father—throw yourfelf at his feet—entreat his protection—

Juliana. I will; there is no other hope—go where I will, they ſtill purfue and perfecute me.— Yes! I'll to my father!

Lavifh. Come then—allow me to conduct you— and if I too throw myfelf at his feet, and he no longer thinks me his enemy——

Juliana. Alas! even then, Mr. Lavifh——confider, I am fo deſtitute of every hope of fortune—

Lavifh. Fortune! oh, if that's all the difficulty, it's only to leſſen our expences—to live on a narrow fcale:—inſtead of a houfe in Grofvenor-fquare, we muſt be content with one in Grofvenor-ſtreet:—inſtead of four horfes, we muſt drive only a pair:—and to avoid gaming and giving great entertainments, we muſt go every night to the play or the opera.—But come—and though thus far I ſhall ſtint you, my dear Juliana, in every other refpect I'll indulge you to the laſt ſhilling—I will, if I fave it a thoufand ways!   [*Exeunt.*

THE END OF THE FOURTH ACT.

ACT V.

SCENE—*The Court-yard of a Prifon; Wall and great Gates in back Scene; on each Side Apartments in the Prifon, and O. P. Steps leading up to a Door.— Moonlight.*

Sir HERVEY *and* WORRY *difcovered.*

Worry. Nay, let me entreat you, Sir, retire to your chamber!—you forget you are in a prifon.

Sir Hervey. But are you fure my daughter is not Alltrade's wife?

Worry. I am, Sir! and that fhe owes her deliverance to the generous exertions of Captain Lavifh. (*Loud knocking at gate.*)—There—you hear, Sir! —now pray, pray retire.

Sir Hervey. Well! conduct me; and in the morning wait on Captain Lavifh, and exprefs my warmeft gratitude.—

Worry. Aye, that I will, Sir! and make everv inquiry after Mifs Sutherland:— but now, Sir! (*Loud knocking again*).—Blefs me! this is a moft unconfcionable fort of place!—neither let people in or out!—'tis devilifh hard :—I dare fay the gentleman has as much right to be here as anv bod; !— This way, Sir, this way! (Sir HERVEY *and* WORRY *afcend fteps, and exeunt.*)

F

Gates

(Gates are opened, and enter JULIANA *and two Bailiffs.)*

Firſt Bailiff. Come, come!—now all's ſafe:—though if we hadn't contrived to ſeparate her from Captain Laviſh by means of a forged letter—

Second Bailiff. Ay, that was my planning!—ſo here you are, Miſs! arreſted on your bond for five thouſand pounds ;—and you know Mr. Alltrade's terms!—either ſign a contraᏧ of marriage——

Juliana. That I never will.

Firſt Bailiff. Good night then.

Juliana. Stay!—ſpare me but a moment!—unuſed to this ſcene of terror and diſtreſs, unleſs ſome friendly hand is ſtretched to ſave me, I muſt e'en fall and periſh here !—Oh, I am faint ! quite—quite ſick at heart.

Second Bailiff. You'd better ſign the contraᏧ then.

Juliana. Never ! never ! *(Bailiffs exeunt)*.—They're. gone :—now, Juliana, ſummon all your courage !—alone,—unproteᏧed ! in the worſt place, amongſt the worſt ſociety ; ſeparated from the man you love, deſerted by the father you revere, and ſo deprived of every hope of aid, that, ſhould you linger on for years, here, here at laſt muſt be your grave ! *(Shouting and laughing without.)*—Heavens ! what noiſe is that ?—a ſet of the moſt needy and moſt deſperate! *(Stamping :)* Again !—they come this way—and I am left to be the viᏧim of their brutality !—I can't ſupport it !—I faint with terror !—Oh, help ! help ! *(Falls at the foot of the ſteps)*.

Re-enter

Re-enter Sir HERVEY.

Sir Hervey. Surely I heard a woman's voice,—
and feemingly in much diftrefs!—'tis fo!—poor
wretch!—fhe fcarcely breathes:—Within there!
(*Re-enter* Worry:)—give your affiftance! help me
to raife this poor unfortunate.

Worry. I will, I will! (*They raife* JULIANA, *who
remains· in a lifelefs ftate*).— Merciful powers!
(*feeing her face, ftarting, and moving away*).

Sir Hervey. Ha! what alarms you?—do you
know her?

Worry. I do!

Sir Hervey. Who is it?—what brings her here?
fpeak!—has fhe no friends? no relations?

Worry. Yes:—fhe has a father!

Sir Hervey. Barbarian!—could he not prevent—

Worry. He could, but————afk your own
heart! mine would burft to fpeak it.

Sir Hervey. How?

Worry. Ay, your much wronged daughter!—who
evidently has been brought here on the bond fhe
figned to fave you!—but don't—don't be unhappy, Sir! I'll go directly for affiftance.

Sir Hervey. Fly! begone! (WORRY *exit.*—JULI-
ANA *remains ftill lifelefs in* Sir HERVEY'S *arms:*)—
can I behold all this, and live?—Poor girl!—the
very features of————Oh, God! Oh, God!

Juliana. Give me air!—So; I am much, much
better.

Sir Hervey. Indeed!—I am glad, cordially
glad: ha! ha! (*weeping*)—you've faved my life!

Juliana. Your life!—fuch kindnefs from a ftranger!—Oh! in this place I little thought to find a
friend!

Sir

Sir Hervey. And do you call me friend!

Juliana. I hope I may! you feem to take an intereft in my fufferings.

Sir Hervey. I do—I do! and well I know the author of them all!—too well I know the father that has caufed them.

Juliana. My father! do you know my father?—Oh, when you fee him, don't tell him you found me in prifon! that would afflict him, and it would double my mifery to add to his!—don't—pray don't tell him, Sir.

Sir Hervey. Why not?—why feel for him who never felt for you! has he not from your infancy deferted you?—has he not fhut his doors againft you? and, inftead of being your friend and protector, has he not proved himfelf your enemy—your perfecutor?

Juliana (haughtily). Well! if he has, Sir?

Sir Hervey. Did he not thwart you in your affections,—tear you from the man you love, and command you to marry him you hate?—and after thefe accumulated injuries, and you had involved yourfelf to fupport him, what was his return? ingratitude! what was your inheritance? poverty!—what has been your reward? a prifon!—Oh, villain! villain!—worft of villains!

Juliana. Villain!—hold your unlicenfed tongue. Villain!—who are you that dare thus accufe my father?

Sir Hervey. A libertine; whofe diffipation drove his wife into fuch fcenes of error and remorfe that fhe died of a broken heart!—an outcaft! who, not content with that, would have reduced his daughter to the fame unhappy fate!—a wretch! who, abandoned her not for her own conduct, but her mother's!—who brought her to a prifon!—who

fees

fees her there without the hope of faving her!—or, to fum up all in one emphatic word—to give the aggregate of complicated infamy——I am your father!

Juliana. My father!

Sir Hervey. Ay, look at me!—view me well—do you not fhudder at the hideous fight?. will you not curfe—avoid me as a peftilence?—a fiend!

Juliana. No: I will cling to you!—thus grow for ever round you! *(throwing herfelf into his* arms).—My father! my dear, dear father!

Sir Hervey. Juliana, be merciful!—load me with reproaches—this kindnefs will deftroy me!

Juliana. Reproach you!—what, at the moment I have found you?—no: let me but be near you, and I will blefs the hour that brought me to this place!—for it has given me the utmoft wifhes of my foul—it has reftored to me a parent!

Enter ALLTRADE *and* WORRY.

Worry. There! 'tis as I expected; they are re-conciled—look! have you the heart to interrupt their joy?

Alltrade. Sir Hervey, I have no wifh but to give you both liberty; and if you will fulfil your promife, by perfuading Mifs Sutherland to accept my hand——nay: why frown?—you fee I come as a friend.

Sir Hervey. Friend! away—I'm weary of the very word.

Alltrade. What! weary of friendfhip, Sir Hervey!

Sir Hervey. Ay, Sir; time was, when friend-fhip wore a bold and open afpect, and as it fpoke

it

it acted: but now 'tis masked; and underneath it
lurks all modern villany. Who betrayed my wife?
a friend!—who belied my child? a friend!—
who immured her in a gaol, and if she does not
prostitute her hand and heart, will fee her pe-
rish there—who, but my friend!—Can my enemy
thus injure me?—No; in him I place no confi-
dence or trust; and henceforth let me rather meet
a thousand foes than the designing arts of one false
friend.

Alltrade. Well, as you please—*(Enter* LAVISH
behind)—here is Miss Sutherland's discharge; but
since you don't choose to accede to my proposals,
good night *(shewing discharge, and putting it up
again).*

Juliana. Nay, let me entreat you, Mr. Alltrade.

Worry. And let me entreat you, Mr. Alltrade.

Alltrade. No, I can be obstinate in my turn—
good night.

Lavish (advancing and turning ALLTRADE
round). Then let me entreat you, Mr. Alltrade—
nay, don't think to escape, Sir—Bless you! you
are quite mistaken; Mr. Alltrade's the most kind,
obliging——The discharge—give me the discharge,
you scoundrel—or else, Newmarket in the first
place *(shaking his cane),* and high life in the second *(pulling up his neckcloth).*

Alltrade (trembling violently). Well, Sir—
since you insist, Sir—

Lavish. I do; and be quick—dispatch—(ALL-
TRADE *gives* LAVISH *a paper).* Oh, this is the very
thing I suppose—*(begins reading it)*—" By this
" my last will, I Jeremiah Dazzle give and be-
" queath"——

                                        Alltrade.

Alltrade. Stop, ſtop—that's the wrong paper—here, here's the diſcharge.

Laviſh (takes it and puts it into his pocket). Very well—a good economiſt pockets every thing—*(Reads on)* : " all the property of which I die poſ-" ſeſſed, unto that moſt amiable——Juliana " Sutherland."——Amazement ! *(Sir* HERVEY, JULIANA, *and* LAVISH *all look at each other with aſtoniſhment, and during pauſe* ALLTRADE *exit.)* There—you take care of that, Sir Hervey, whilſt I take care of Mr.—*(turns round and finds* ALL-TRADE *gone)*—what ! gone !—I'll follow him—I'll ——but no—we've got all we want from him—and ſo, 'ſpite of our former animoſities, Sir Hervey, allow me to congratulate you.

Sir Hervey (having read the will). No, Sir ; my hopes are vaniſhed, I find here the fortune is conditional :—if my daughter marries, it devolves to Mrs. Dazzle.

Laviſh. If ſhe marries ?

Sir Hervey. Ay, Sir !—while ſhe remains ſingle, ſhe may roll in affluence, and I be reſtored to all my former ſplendor ;—but will that give either of us con-ſolation ? No ; my own ſad example has taught me the reverſe ; and therefore, mark me, Juliana—I wiſh to make atonement, to give you fixed, un-ceaſing happineſs ;—and having proved myſelf un-fit to guard ſo dear a charge,—let him who beſt deſerves, let him proteſt you !

Juliana. Him !—whom, Sir ?

Sir *Hervey (pointing to* LAVISH). Him !—Ac-cept her, Mr. Laviſh,—take her as the beſt re-compence for all the wrongs I've done you.—Nay, I know the penalty :—I know, by marrying you ſhe forfeits this eſtate ; and for your ſake I wiſh it had accompanied her ; but for my own !—at laſt

I've

I've acted as a parent ought, and though these
gates are ever shut against me, I know my daughter's happy, and that thought will give what wealth
can never purchase;—a quiet confcience and un-
broken reft.

Lavish. Sir Hervey, you have acted nobly—
but——

Sir Hervey. But what?—You are fufficiently
affluent to maintain her.

Lavish. No; there's the curfe on't : I thought
I had faved a fortune ;—but juft now, when I heard
of your mutual diftrefs, and drew bills on my
fteward and my banker, they refufed payment ;—
to my aftonifhment they faid I hadn't a fhilling!—there you fee, there's the end of my economy!

Sir Hervey. And you'd have paid my debts—
you'd have releafed your enemy?

Lavish. Ay, that I would, if I'd faved it a thoufand ways;—but to marry on fuch conditions!—
No—I'll die firft.

Juliana. And fo will I ; and hard as it is, here
let us feparate, Mr. Lavifh.

Sir Hervey. Never!—never fhall you be divided!
—and though we can expect no liberality from
Mrs. Dazzle, yet under all the circumftances fhe
may be induced to compromife—perhaps allow
us a moiety, or a third.

Lavish. Ay, or any thing,—if fhe'll only allow
us two hundred a-year, with my management I'll
be bound we'll all live comfortably ;—I'll go make
her propofals inftantly, and don't fear my fuccefs;
—for at a bargain,—never was fuch a fellow at
making a bargain.

Juliana. Adieu, Mr. Lavifh ; pray Heaven
you may fucceed!

Worry.

Worry. So fay I; and if fhe don't come to an amicable adjuftment, conteft the will, and employ my nephew to file a bill in Chancery againft her.

Lavifh. No, that will never do : rather give up the whole property than go to law.—Come, that's good economy, or the devil's in it.   [*Exit.*

Sir Hervey. Come, Juliana, in my apartments we'll wait his return.—(*To* WORRY): You alfo, faithful, conftant friend !

Juliana. How fhall I thank you ? how repay—

Worry. Repay !—Look ! are you not reconciled ? Isn't that repaying me ?—Oh ! I am the happieft fellow living !——No—I forgot Mrs. Worry.

[*Exeunt* O. P.

SCENE—*A Street in the Town.*

Enter ALLTRADE, Mrs. DAZZLE, *and a* Servant.

Mrs. Dazzle. Don't talk to me, Sir.—The will difcovered !

Alltrade. I tell you it was no fault of mine, and my life on't Mifs Sutherland will marry the Captain, and ftill forfeit the bequeft.

Mrs. Dazzle. She marry ! fhe marry ! non- fenfe ! Haven't I this inftant feen the faithlefs Cap- tain, and isn't it exactly as I fufpected ?—Take my word for it, Juliana will keep the eftate and her lover too.

Alltrade. How ! what mean you ?

Mrs. Dazzle. Mean ? that the Captain never thought of making her his wife ; and the father, to gain his liberty and five thoufand a-year, will be

                                                           unprin-

unprincipled enough to confent to his daughter's difgrace.

Alltrade. Oh, I underftand now:—live together without marrying.

Mrs. Dazzle. Ay; Mr. Lavifh not only didn't deny the infamous fcheme, but abfolutely offered me two hundred a-year if I'd give up all claim under my hufband's will; if not, he faid he and Juliana would go to Italy, and live on the profits. What fhall I do?—deprived of my hufband's eftate, I'm abfolutely pennylefs.

Alltrade. I know; and you fee they are decided; therefore, why hefitate?—two hundred a-year is certainly better than nothing.

Mrs. Dazzle. True; and as I have no other hope,—John, go to Mr. Lavifh, fay I accede to his propofals, and if he'll bring an agreement to my houfe, I'll fign directly. (*Servant exit.*) Oh! that it fhould come to this;—but I'll expofe them— I'll——

Enter STOPGAP (*with a letter*).

Stopgap. From Mr. Mift, Madam;—it is of the utmoft confequence, and requires an immediate anfwer (*giving letter*).

Mrs. Dazzle. Indeed!

Stopgap. Yes, Madam;—he has this moment received pofitive information, that Mr. Dazzle died poffeffed of half a London theatre; and as you are his widow, Madam—but the letter will explain.

Mrs. Dazzle (reading). " Majeftic Mrs. M. P.
" —only time to fay, forget paft bad management
" —accept hand and fortune; we'll inftantly act
" Benedict

" Benedict and Beatrice.—Doors to be opened at
" eight, and performance begin precisely at nine.
" Vivant Rex et Regina!—P. M. ——. *N. B.*
" Would have waited on you in person, but
" Harlequin and flow waggon are just arrived."
Delightful! glorious!—now I am rich enough to
defy the Captain and his associates:—My compliments to Mr. Mist, I'll wait upon him instantly,
and the sooner the marriage takes place, the happier it will make me. (STOPGAP *exit.*)—Come, Mr.
Alltrade, you shall share my good fortune, and
when the Captain brings the agreement, how I
shall laugh at him; I now despise, as much as I
once loved him. [*Exeunt.*

SCENE—*Inside of a Theatre.*

MIST *discovered.*

Mist. Forfeit 'em,—I'll forfeit 'em.—Harlequin
arrived!—first call new pantomime, and not an
actor come to rehearsal;—vagabonds!—all envy
—all jealousy;—dread his immortal powers, and
want to knock him up;—won't do though—not
easily put out of countenance.

Enter STOPGAP.

Stopgap. Joy! I give you joy, Sir; Mrs.
Dazzle consents.
Mist. What! doors opened at eight.
Stop. Ay, and performance begin at nine.
Mist.

Mifl. And no money returned after curtain's drawn up!—tol de roll, toll, loll :—I'm a real London Manager !—that, (*fnapping his fingers,*) that for this half or rather no priced toy-fhop:—but where is fhe ?—where's the imperial Mrs. M. P.

Stopgap. She'll be here directly, and Mr. Squib alfo: I met him in the ftreet, and on my telling him you were about to marry Mrs. Dazzle for the fake of her theatrical property, he faid you were grofsly impofed upon, and that he'd wait upon you, and explain the matter inftantly :—and fee, here he comes.

Mifl. He explain! pfha! what does he know about—(*Enter* LAVISH)—Excufe me, Mr. Squib, can't talk to ftrollers now; I'm real—a Royal London Manager.

Lavifh. So am I; I'm a real Royal London Manager.

Mifl. You!—good, very good; and you've got old Dazzle's fhare, fuppofe?

Lavifh. Yes, and I've got old Dazzle's fhare, fuppofe.

Mifl. Better and better!—in right of the heirefs too?

Lavifh. Yes, in right of the heirefs too.

Mifl. What, you mean to marry the widow?

Lavifh. No, damn me if I do; and if I did, that wouldn't help me.

Mifl. No!

Lavifh. No; the theatre is not hers, it belongs to Mifs Sutherland—(*producing will*) :—here it is under old Dazzle's hand : here's another apology, read it, and then once more—" Ladies and Gentle-" men, the difagreeable dilemma to which I " am reduced"—ha! ha! there's a Manager for you !

Mrs.

Mrs. Dazzle (without). Where is my life, my lord, my hufband?

Lavifh. There, you read the will, while I talk to the *heirefs.*—(MIST *and* STOPGAP *retire up the ſtage with the will,* Mrs. DAZZLE *enters.*)—So, widow, here's the agreement.

Mrs. Dazzle. Then you may take it back again; I fhan't fign it.

Lavifh. No!

Mrs. Dazzle. No; my marriage with Mr. Miſt makes me fufficiently rich and independent to refufe the paltry offer; and I can now fhew the world that I'm above being a party in fo infamous a tranfaction! fo I wifh you a pleafant tour to Italy, good Signor Lavifhini.

Lavifh. You're wrong! it's a mighty pretty income:—I'd be bound to keep a carriage on two hundred a-year.

Mrs. Dazzle. Very likely: but you have your anfwer, Sir.

Stopgap (behind to MIST). Yes: Mifs Sutherland's heirefs!—Mr. Squib Manager.

Miſt. And I'm dethroned:—exit Miſt.

Mrs. Dazzle. Look! there's my dear intended! Now, Sir, fee me take pofleffion of his hand and ate.—Oh, Mr. Miſt! (*curtfeying.*)

Stopgap (afide to MIST). I have a thought, Sir! rhaps Mifs Sutherland may wifh to fell—and ᵗʰrough Mr. Squib's intereft, and by fecuring him the deputyfhip—

Miſt. I may get purchafe! well prompted, Stop— we'll pay court to new monarch;—now mind, one of beft benefit bows.—(*They put themfelves in bowing attitudes and advance towards* Mrs. DAZZLE.)

Mrs. Dazzle. Delightful man!—with what awe he approaches me!—you fee, Signor—you fee!
(MIST

(Mist *and* Stopgap *pafs by* Mrs. Dazzle *and come clofe to* Lavish.)

Mift. Royal Mr. Squib—fee your authority, and humbly—

Mrs. Dazzle (turning him round). Why, Mr. Mift, I'm on this fide.

Mift. I know! but I am on the other fide: a good Manager always goes with the ruling party:—any reparation to you or the heirefs, Mr. Squib! would fhe choofe the freedom? or you take a benefit?—play myfelf, and give you firft night of new pantomime.

Lavifh. You fee, Signora, you fee!—why if you're in earneft, Mr. Mift, Mifs Sutherland's father is in prifon, and as this Will gives him no ready money—

Mift. I take—what's the debt?

Lavifh. A trifle!—but a thoufand pounds, which in the courfe of a month I can fave and repay you!—or if that fecurity don't content you, you fhall have a mortgage on the theatre.

Mift. That's it; that's the beft fecurity on earth! far better than meadows and corn fields!—people will go without bread, but, blefs 'em! never without plays!—Come along, Stop—prifon only next door—gaoler take my word:—re enter with Sir Hervey inftantly.

Mrs. Dazzle. Why, are you mad, Sir?—will you again difappoint and deceive me?

Mift. Deceive you!—hem!—who concealed will?—paffed off for Manager, and turns out only author?—who under falfe pretences would have pocketed all my fcenes, dreffes, and decorations?—No, no—you deceived me; and therefore, " Mary, " once more I follow thee! and fo, Good morrow, " good Queen Elizabeth!" [*Exit with* Stopgap.

Mrs.

Mrs. Dazzle. Barbarian! Savage!—this is the third time he has made a dupe of me, Mr. Lavifh! (*Burfts into tears*).—I'll fign the agreement, Mr. Lavifh!

Lavifh. Excufe me!—I'm above being a party in fo infamous a tranfaction.

Mrs. Dazzle. Nay: when you confider the fmallnefs of the fum, and that I bind myfelf to give up all claim under my hufband's will.—

Lavifh. Why, that's true; and ferioufly fpeaking two hundred a-year is no object; and therefore, I'll indulge you?—fign directly, and I'll indulge you!

Mrs. Dazzle. The fooner the better!—I long to be out of the monfter's houfe!—here's pen and ink.

Lavifh. And here's the agreement! (*they go to the table*).

Enter Mist, Sir Hervey, *and* Juliana.

Mift. Take care—confider you're a new performer, Sir Hervey—you alfo, Mifs M. P. mind the traps.

Sir Hervey. Sir, I know not how to exprefs my thanks or my aftonifhment.

Lavifh (*coming from table—agreement in his hand*). Huzza! Sir Hervey, I give you joy—Mifs Sutherland, I give you joy—here it is, figned and fealed.—Mrs. Dazzle generoufly takes two hundred a-year, and gives up all claim under her hufband's will—there! there's a bargain maker for you!

Sir Hervey. Is this true, Madam?

Mrs. Dazzle. True!—you know I've been tricked into it.

Lavifh. You have—you trick'd yourfelf into it.

Mrs. Dazzle. Myfelf!

Lavifh. Ay! you would be indulged; and as here is now no longer any bar to our union, with this lady's (*taking* JULIANA's *hand*) and her father's leave allow me to introduce you to Mrs. Lavifh elect.

Mrs. Dazzle. How! your wife!

Lavifh. Ay; you thought I'd call her by another name; but I am ftill old fafhioned enough to think the word "wife," heightens happinefs and gives a zeft to love!—(Mrs. DAZZLE *is going to fpeak*)—Nay, don't blame me!—you have to thank yourfelf for the whole tranfaction; and when any body makes falfe charges, I hope I fhall be always too good an economift not to make them pay for them.

Mift (*to* Mrs. DAZZLE). You take the hint!—you take the hint!

Mrs Dazzle. Oh, I fhall go wild—I—(*ftamping violently*).—

Mift. Gently—you'll be down the trap.

Mrs. Dazzle. So, Mifs, you mean to allow me only this paltry——

Juliana. No, Madam!—with my hufband's permiffion the annuity fhall be doubled.—The widow of my benefactor muft be more amply provided for.

Lavifh. Certainly!—I can fave it a thoufand ways!—And now, Mr. Mift, as we fhall certainly difpofe of our theatrical property, you fhall be the purchafer—Only mind, I make the bargain—never was fuch a fellow at making bargains!

Mift. Name your own terms—only let me be London Manager!—Oh, for the opening!—Oh, for the firft night!—After Hamlet, what an addrefs will I make to them?

Lavifh. Addrefs! why what will you fay?

Mift. Tell you—"Ladies and Gentlemen—on " the part of the company in general, and myfelf

" as proprietor, author, actor, and manager in
" particular—confefs faults—acknowledge obliga-
" tions—and humbly entreat your ufual candour
" and indulgence."——Then getting nearer the
lamps—" Ladies and Gentlemen, to-morrow and
" following evening, with your permiffion, this play,
" will be repeated!"

THE END OF THE COMEDY.

EPILOGUE,

WRITTEN BY GEORGE COLMAN, ESQ.

Spoken by Mr. FAWCETT *in the Character of* MIST.

———————

A London Manager of high degree,
I, Peter Mift, now enter here O. P. ;
My country playhoufe, e'er I came to town
Almoft knock'd up, has been in lots knock'd down.
   A fturdy farmer bought the walls :—why then,
What was a barn will be a barn again.
Corn on the ftage, not mummers will be feen ;
And oats bé threfh'd where actors fhould have been ;
Wheat ftrew the boards where erft did heroes tread,
To make—what heroes never made there—bread.
   Stage-ftruck, but hen-peck'd, honeft Juftice Dunder
Has all my clouds,—his lady has my thunder.
Dick Drench, the fnug apothecary, means
To give a private play, fo buys my fcenes :
Drench, " fmelling of the fhop," and *idem femper*,
Could not refift fcenes painted in diftemper.
   The Member for the town bought all my coats ;
There he was wife—for I command two votes ;
And playhoufe coats (again he fhew'd difcerning)
Will fuit a Member, for they're us'd to turning.
   My wigs the women quarrell'd for, fweet fouls !
My daggers ftuck in felling ; but my bowls
Mine hoft of the Red Lion clapp'd his eyes on,
And bought 'em, as I did, to ferve up poifon.
   Thus all my country ftock, as Shakfpeare fays,
   " My cloud-capt towers, my gorgeous palaces,
   " Yea, my great globe," (the barn,) fo much involv'd,
And " all it did inherit, have diffolv'd."
                                            But

But if fome future Manager fhould take
My " folemn temple," which I now forfake ;
My " fabric of a vifion," he will find
That I have left a curfed " wreck behind."
   Here then I come, by rural fchemes half undone,
But country ftumps appear new brooms in London.
Egad I'll fweep all clean—look to't—ne'er doubt me—
A London Manager, I'll lay about me ;
And, as a fample, you fhall hear my hints,
To be inferted in to-morrow's prints :
  " A five act play laft night was reprefented,
" By an amazing *Dramatift* invented !
" Author's and Actors' merits were immenfe,
" And Fawcett e'en furpafs'd his ufual excellence !
" Great care 'tis plain was taken in rehearfal ;
" And"——may I add with *truth ?*——" applaufe was
  " univerfal."

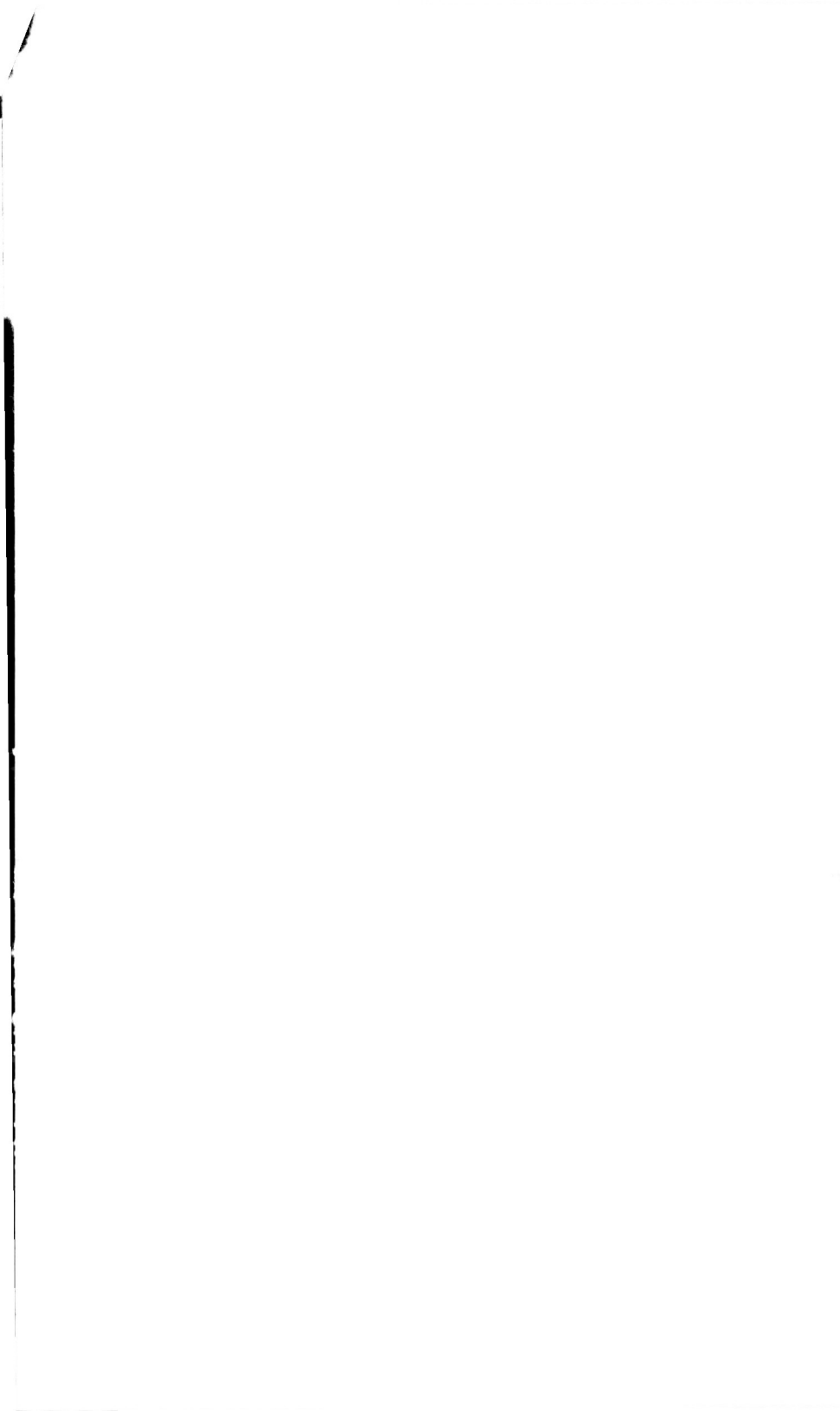

www.ingramcontent.com/pod-product-compliance
Lightning Source LLC
Chambersburg PA
CBHW031449270326
41930CB00007B/926

*9 7 8 3 3 3 7 0 0 5 9 8 6 *